Vietnam Was a Just War

The Evolution of the Cavalry and How it Changed Warfare

Joe Abodeely

Desert Bugle Press
P.O. Box 1065
Maricopa, AZ 85139

ISBN (print) 978-0-9915286-4-6
ISBN (ebook) 978-0-9915286-5-3
LCCN: 2022911207

Special thanks to the Everett Collection, Kent State University,
Jearld Moldenhauer, Robert Lutz, and others for use of their photos.

See page 297 for detailed photo credits.

*Vietnam Was a Just War: The Evolution of the Cavalry
and How it Changed Warfare*
©2022, Joseph E. Abodeely. All rights reserved. v. 1.01

The publisher supports the value of copyright. Copyright fuels creativity, encourages diverse voices, promotes free speech, and creates a vibrant culture. Thank you for purchasing authorized editions of this book and by complying with copyright laws. Scanning, uploading, or distributing this book without permission is a theft of the author's intellectual property. If you would like permission to use material from this book (other than for review purposes) please contact the publisher.

While the information in this book is believed to be true and accurate at the date of publication, neither the author nor the editor nor the publisher can accept any legal responsibility for any errors or omissions that may be made. The publisher makes no warranty, expressed or implied, with respect to the material contained herein. The publisher is not responsible for the websites (or their content) that are not owned by the publisher.

Author exercised reasonable due diligence in determining ownership of photos used in this book. Copyrighted photos are credited. Every effort has been made to trace all copyright holders, but if any have been overlooked, the publisher will be pleased to include any necessary credits in any subsequent reprint or edition.

Vietnam Was a Just War
is available at special quantity discounts when purchased in bulk.
Please email the author at JoeAbo7@gmail.com or visit him on the web at
www.JoeAbo.com for more information.

for those who served in Vietnam

Contents

History of the Vietnam War vii
   Prologue 1
   Historical Comparisons of Wars 13
   Comparisons of Afghanistan and Vietnam Wars 27

Was Vietnam a Just War? 31
   Vietnam Was a Just War 33
   Examples of Major Military Actions 41

History of Air Cavalry 65
   Horses to Helicopters 67
   Air Cavalry in Vietnam 77
   History of Air Mobility 83
   Night Stalkers 89
   Women, Racists, and Dissidents in the Military 95

My Personal Experience in Vietnam 103
   My Introduction to Vietnam 105
   Be Careful What You Wish For 109

The Tet Offensive **113**
　Khe Sanh and the Beginning of Tet 115
　February 27, 1968—My Epiphany 123
　Diary and Recollections About Khe Sanh 139
　Three Accounts of Operation Pegasus 175

The Orthodox Versus the Revisionists **203**
　Why Is the Vietnam War Still Misrepresented? 205
　Vietnam Anti-War Movement 213
　Orthodox Versus Revisionist Views on Vietnam 247
　The Vietnam War Isn't Over 257

Appendix **263**
　Appendix 1 265
　Appendix 2 287
　About the Author 291
　Recommended Reading 293
　Credits 297

Also by Joe Abodeely

Winner of the 2021 Dan Poynter Legacy Award, ***Vietnam Anti-War Movement: The Great American Con Job,*** also won, Best Education in Non-Fiction (gold), Best History in Non-Fiction (gold), Best Military Non-Fiction (gold), Best Ebook Cover (gold).

Dear Mom and Dad, Love from Vietnam
Winner of three Global E-book Awards, 2014: Best History in Non-Fiction (gold), Best Autobiography / Memoirs Non-Fiction (bronze), Best in Military Non-Fiction (gold).

History of the Vietnam War

Six U.S. Presidents, Truman, Eisenhower, Kennedy, Johnson, Nixon, and Ford, supported South Vietnam against the Communist invasion against South Vietnam.

Prologue

Many who opposed the Vietnam War claimed it was not a "just war." Considering relevant factors, Vietnam was more of a "just war" than many other wars.

In 1951-52, the U.S. first sent military assistance and advisors to Vietnam to stop the spread of Communism. U.S. forces ended fighting in 1973 and did not leave until 1975. Vietnam (not Afghanistan) was the longest war in U.S. history to date.

Overview of the Vietnam War

America wanted to stop the spread of Communism because—1) Joseph Stalin and Mao Zedong's pledge to support Ho Chi Minh's Viet Minh guerrillas (Viet Cong) against French colonization, 2) U.S. domestic pressure to act against Communism after the loss of mainland China in WW II, and 3) the indecisive conclusion of the Korean War.

In May 1950, President Truman committed 10 million U.S. dollars in military aid and formed the Defense Attaché Office in Saigon to support anti-Communist forces in the Republic of Vietnam (RVN).

In September 1950, Truman sent the Military Assistance Advisory Group (MAAG) to Vietnam to assist the French in the First Indochina War claiming they were not sent as combat troops but to supervise the use of $10 million worth of US military equipment sent to support the French in their effort to fight the Viet Minh forces.

In 1951-52, U.S. military assistance and advisors were sent to Vietnam. Truman's position was that the U.S. was helping the Vietnamese stop Communism rather than helping the French keep a colony. The Viet Minh gained extensive popular support since its inception in 1941; and this resistance continued as the French and U.S. tried to reoccupy Vietnam.

In 1953, President Dwight D. Eisenhower saw the fall of French Indochina and the threat of Communist expansion in Southeast Asia as the Domino Theory (e.g., if South Vietnam fell, all Southeast Asia would fall). U.S. military aid jumped above $350 million and replaced the badly worn World War II vintage equipment that France was using because it was still suffering economically from the devastation of that war.

The French Army was reluctant to take U.S. advice and would not allow the Vietnamese army to be trained with the new equipment because it went against French policy. French commanders were possessive of their historic colonial role and thwarted MAAG attempts to observe where the equipment was sent and how it was used. Eventually, the French cooperated, but it was too late.

On May 7, 1954, France lost control over the South when the Viet Minh defeated the French at Dien Bin Phu. The Geneva Agreement, signed on July 20, 1954, ended the colonial war, granted independence to South Vietnam, and divided Vietnam at the 17th parallel pending unifying elections to be held in 1956. Ngo Dinh Diem returned at Bao Dai's request to be prime minister of a U.S.-backed government which would be proclaimed the Republic of Vietnam (South Vietnam).

In September 1954, the Southeast Asia Treaty Organization (SEATO) was formed with the U.S., France, Great Britain, New Zealand, Australia, the Philippines, Thailand, and Pakistan—all desiring to protect the region.

Several thousand Communist VC (Viet Minh) defied the terms of the Geneva Accords, remained underground in South Vietnam, and terrorized the populace. The U.S. blocked the elections from happening because South Vietnam feared Communist political and dissident groups would disrupt voting and make an unfair election.

President Eisenhower wrote to Diem, the new Prime Minister of the Bao Dai government promising U.S. support to preserve a non-Communist Vietnam.

In January 1955, the U.S. began direct aid to South Vietnam as Diem suppressed religious sects in the Mekong Delta and unrest in Saigon to consolidate control. In February, U.S. advisors arrived to train the South Vietnamese army. In October, in a government-controlled referendum, Diem defeated and ousted the emperor Bao Dai and made himself president of South Vietnam.

In 1956, Diem refused to follow the 1954 Geneva Accords which called for free elections in all of Vietnam. He created an autocratic regime because he thought the Communists would intimidate voters and deny a free election.

In 1957, prior to increased U.S. involvement in Vietnam, a small peace movement arose, mostly concerned about nuclear testing. It was primarily led by the Committee for Sane Nuclear Policy (SANE), created by and including the Committee for Nonviolent Action (CNVA), founded that same year, and Women's Strike for Peace (WSP).

The early opposition to the war was largely restricted to pacifists and leftists empowered by strategic nonviolent action in the U.S. Civil Rights Movement.

Students for a Democratic Society (SDS) emerged in 1960, promoting democratic socialism and opposition to the war. Many joined the Reserve or National Guard to avoid Vietnam and later called themselves "Vietnam era veterans."

In December 1960, the Viet Cong was the military arm of the National Liberation Front (NLF), an underground Communist insurgency. It was formed to be active in South Vietnam to terrorize and infiltrate the Vietnamese people under Diem.

In May 1961, President John F. Kennedy sent 500 more military advisers to Vietnam, increasing American forces to 1,400. The increased budget and American boots on the ground caused some in the U.S. government and others in the U.S. general populace to begin to question these actions.

In May 1963, Diem, an ardent Roman Catholic, did

not accede to various demands from the Buddhists, who claimed religious discrimination. Communists infiltrated and agitated the age-old conflict between Catholics and Buddhists. There were mass Buddhist protests and allegations that Diem's police killed Buddhist protesters after the police received gunfire. The journalists thought Diem was not liberal enough in dealing with the press and Buddhist protesters.

U.S. journalists did not believe Diem's denial nor his claim that the Communists infiltrated the Buddhists and started the shooting. Buddhists were outraged, and some of Diem's Buddhist generals called the U.S. to request permission to "remove" Diem.

On November 1, 1963, President John F. Kennedy approved the generals' request; and they assassinated Diem and his brother in a successful *coup d'état* that ended nine years of autocratic rule and nepotism under Diem. The Communists later admitted they started the conflict. The region became more unstable in his absence. Three weeks later, JFK was assassinated.

In August 1964, President Lyndon Baynes Johnson expanded U.S. troop increases and began a bombing campaign against North Vietnam; but American public opinion did not want the U.S. involved in Vietnam. Since there was a draft, every eligible young man faced fighting in the jungles of Vietnam. The antiwar movement grew; and the draft, not a keen understanding of geopolitics, fueled the antiwar movement. Television thrived on promoting antiwar views.

In 1964, the first major U.S. protests began and gained strength as the war escalated. Military recruiters and Dow Chemical (chief manufacturer of napalm) were often met by protesters at the campuses. At the University of Michigan, "teach-ins" on the Vietnam War modeled after Civil Rights Movement seminars brought in thousands of people to Washington, D.C. Opposition to the war increased as body counts escalated, civilian atrocities reports circulated, draft calls increased, and the prospects for a U.S. victory dissipated.

Conscription impacted working and middle-class families and helped mobilize college students who faced being sent to Vietnam soon after graduation. Draft-dodging was not based on a keen sense of geopolitical understanding, but rather on self-preservation. Civil disobedience—public burning of draft cards, sit-ins on the steps of the Pentagon, draft induction centers, and railroad tracks transporting troops gradually increased. The Civil Rights and Black Power Movements, antiwar protests, and television, helped shape public opinion against the war.

In 1967, 300,000 marched in New York City and 50,000 protesters were at the Pentagon, with over 700 being arrested. A national organization of draft resisters was formed in 1967 calling itself the "Resistance." Many thousands were jailed, some went to Canada, or went underground. Opposition to the war increased as body counts escalated, civilian atrocities reports circulated, draft calls increased, and the media reported that prospects of a U.S. "victory" dissipated.

By the end of 1967, public support for the war dropped to one-third of the population as media coverage was unsympathetic. Surveillance, smear campaigns, and staged support rallies were organized by government agencies to slow the growth of the Vietnam antiwar movement which was unprecedented in scope. The nomination of pro-war candidates for Presidency further radicalized the anti-war movement and violent police actions against anti-war protesters at the Chicago DNC.

In 1968 and 1969, the Vietnam War death count rose; antiwar protests increased in the U.S. as awareness of the death toll in the nightly TV news reports dejected Americans. Television exploitation of U.S. "massacres" of Vietnamese civilians, torture of political prisoners in South Vietnam, and domestic spying on

U.S. citizens inflamed the U.S. public and drove it further from U.S. government policy.

The news media was more skeptical in its war coverage, and mainstream churches and unions spoke out more boldly. Blockades of thoroughfares and other nonviolent, direct action increased because violent protests alienated most Americans from the anti-war cause.

A countercultural group called the Yippies staged innovative actions and guerrilla theater. Radical priests raided offices of draft boards destroying records. Prominent civil rights leaders, including Martin Luther King, Jr., Jane Fonda, and John Kerry, spoke against the war, while Vietnamese monks immolated themselves protesting the Diem regime. Communist-front groups protested in the U.S. while Jewish lawyers, Catholic priests, Buddhist monks, "Black panthers," gays, labor, women-libbers, draft-age males, and other civil rights groups and activists supported the anti-war movement. In October 1969, three million people were part of the Moratorium on the War across the country, half a million protested in Washington, D.C. in November, and the Johnson administration was forced to begin peace talks with the NVA and VC and to suspend the bombing of North Vietnam.

In the Spring of 1970, President Nixon hoped troop withdrawals and a decline in draft rolls would diminish the anti-war movement, but the U.S. Cambodia invasion caused large-scale protests, military mutinies and desertions which hurt prosecuting the war. Other disruptions forced U.S. ground forces to withdraw from Cambodia less than eight weeks after the initial invasion.

The U.S. government and anti-war crowd tensions against each other escalated when six college students were killed and dozens wounded in demonstrations at Kent State University and Jackson State University. Hundreds of colleges and universities shut down from student strikes and occupations of campus buildings.

In April 1971, three-quarters of a million people marched on Washington; and in May 1971, tens of thousands of protesters attempted to shut down government operations in the nation's capital by blockading bridges and thoroughfares.

On July 26, 1971, Kissinger announced plans for $7.5 billion in aid to be provided for Vietnam and the removal of all U.S. troops within nine months.

In 1972, despite a brief upsurge in protests and resumption of the "air war" in North Vietnam, the anti-war movement morphed into factions; and the withdrawal of most U.S. forces led to fewer protests.

Vietnam Was A Just War

On January 13, 1972—Nixon announced plans for 70,000 U.S. troops (half of the remaining forces) to be pulled out of Vietnam.

On February 21, Nixon met Mao Zedong face to face. On April 20, Nixon announced plans to reduce U.S. troops in South Vietnam to 49,000 by July 1.

On August 29, Nixon announced the further withdrawal of U.S. troops in South Vietnam to only 27,000 by December 1.

In January 1973, the anti-war movement pushed the United States to sign the Paris Peace Accords, end the draft, and withdraw its remaining forces from South Vietnam in 60 days.

Nixon and North Vietnam also agreed to withdraw troops from Cambodia and Laos. On March 29, 1973, the last U.S. combat troops left Vietnam.

On August 9, 1974—Richard Nixon resigned due to "Watergate"; Gerald Ford succeeded him.

In April 1975, NVA Soviet-made tanks reached the Saigon President's palace defeating South Vietnam after the U.S. forces left. As the historian, Baron Von Clausewitz, said, *"War is not an independent phenomenon, but the continuation of politics by different means."*

Martin Luther King, Black Power, Civil Rights Movement, Women's Liberation Movement, Gay Rights

Joe Abodeely

Movement, Farm Workers Movement—the "anti-war" movement—all became the so-called "history of the war."

Historical Comparisons of Wars

Robert Neer, a historian, entrepreneur, and attorney, had a J.D.-Ph.D. from Columbia University and taught in the Hstory Department and Core Curriculum. He was co-founder and co-editor of BlueMassGroup.com, the most widely read political blog in New England. Neer thought that academic historians, mainly those at the nation's most ***richly endowed research universities, largely ignored the history of the U.S military*** and further opined that, as we neglected to study our military, we reduced our ability to understand it and weakened ourselves. There is an old saw that the U.S. military always fights the last war.

Neer's point was perceptive because the U.S. had various foreign interests, enemies, and international obligations requiring use of its military since its beginning as a nation. New threats emerge, and the reasons for and use of the military have changed based on the geopolitics of the times. U.S. tactics, organizations, and missions should adapt to the times, too.

Geopolitics has been defined as:

- the study or the application of the influence of political and economic geography on the politics, national power, foreign policy, etc., of a state.

- the combination of geographic and political factors influencing or delineating a country or region.

- a national policy based on the interrelation of politics and geography.

The following synopses demonstrates America's actions in controversial conflicts.

The American Revolutionary War began with the Battle of Lexington on April 19, 1775, and lasted until September 3, 1783. The fighting took place primarily in North America as American colonists, supported by France and Spain, ultimately achieved independence from Great Britain. *The British considered the colonists as rebels, traitors, and terrorists*, but the colonists won the war. *The United States of America was created out of* *an insurrection* and the Declaration of Independence on July 4, 1776. Wars are like beauty—they are in the eyes of the beholder.

During the **Civil War**, on March 4, 1865, the nation braced itself for the end as thousands of spectators gathered near the U.S. Capitol to hear President Lincoln's second inaugural address. It was a controversial war (just like Vietnam), and Lincoln pleaded:

> *"…let us strive on to finish the work we are in, to bind up the nation's wounds, to care for him who shall have borne the battle and for his widow, and his orphan…"*

Some opine that the Civil War was about economics (North vs. South); others say it was about slavery. Others know it as the "war of Yankee aggression." For his efforts to unify the U.S., Lincoln was assassinated; thousands of Americans died, and racial tensions (Black vs. White) still exist. Some Southerners still do not accept the Civil War's end while waiting for "the South to rise again." The reasons for war can be complex.

World War I began on July 28, 1914. Throughout the war, the U.S. vowed to stay neutral even after several U.S. ships were sunk by German submarines. German forces sunk a British passenger vessel carrying over 1,000 people including Americans. *Enraged American citizens pressured the government to take part in the war.* After Germany stated it would continue to attack passenger ships, the U.S finally joined the allies and entered the war which ended two years later with the Treaty of Versailles. The "war to end all wars" did not do so.

World War II was a dynamic event in the 20th century. There was a strong Nazi movement in the U.S. in the late 1930s, but President Roosevelt maintained U.S. neutrality regarding military actions in Europe. Adolph Hitler came to power, attacked Germany's neighbors, and threatened Britain. Meanwhile, Japan, an ally with Italy and Germany, attacked Pearl Harbor and lit the dynamite of WW II causing U.S. entry into the world war on the side of the Allies.

Roosevelt had warnings of the Japanese attack on Pearl Harbor beforehand and ignored them, but *the attack gave justification for the U.S. to enter the war*. After extensive fighting in Europe, and horrendous action on the Western front against the relentless Japanese, *President Truman authorized using two atomic bombs on the Japanese civilians to finally end the war*—arguably war crimes under the Law of War.

WW II did not create America's "greatest generation." Their offspring were America's greatest generation—the "baby-boomers," who were *self-indulgent, irreverent, vulgar, hedonistic, creative, anti-racist, antimisogynistic, vocal, sensitive, pacifistic,* **and patriots who served in Vietnam**. They created **bad** and **good** change in America.

Korea was a United Nations' operation led primarily by the U.S. to help ***stop the spread of North Korean Communism***. North Korea invaded South Korea following clashes along the border and rebellions in South Korea. China and the Soviet Union supported North Korea while South Korea was supported by the United Nations, principally the United States. The fighting ended with an armistice on July 27, 1953.

Similarly, the **Vietnam War** was another war to stop the spread of Communism—a view supported by Dwight David Eisenhower who had been the Supreme Allied Commander in WW II. The Vietnam War was not the only war with controversial issues. Actions in Iraq and Afghanistan received a "pass" on serious public criticism although their justifications were dubious as thousands of innocent people were killed and billions of dollars was expended. War is messy.

Iraq, according to allegations of the Bush administration, had a weapons of mass destruction (WMD) program that posed a threat to the United States, and Saddam Hussein was supposedly harboring and supporting al-Qaeda—*all false*. Bush administration officials made numerous claims about a purported Hussein–al-Qaeda relationship and WMDs that were based on sketchy evidence rejected by intelligence officials.

The Iraq War began on March 20, 2003, when the US, joined by the UK, Australia, and Poland, launched a "shock and awe" bombing campaign. Iraqi forces were quickly overwhelmed as coalition forces swept through the country. The rationale for war faced heavy criticism, domestically and internationally. The invasion led to the collapse of Saddam Hussein and his capture during Operation Red Dawn in December of that same year. He was executed three years later.

In 2004, the 9/11 Commission concluded there was no evidence of any relationship between Hussein's regime and al-Qaeda. When interrogated by the FBI, Saddam Hussein confirmed that Iraq did not have weapons of mass destruction prior to the US invasion.

In 2005 in the aftermath of the invasion, Iraq held multi-party elections. In 2006, Nouri al-Maliki became Prime Minister and remained in office until 2014. His government enacted policies that alienated the country's previously dominant Sunni minority and worsened sectarian tensions.

Following Hussein's demise, the power vacuum and Coalition Provisional Authority mismanagement led to widespread civil war between Shias and Sunnis, and a lengthy insurgency against coalition forces. Many of the violent insurgent groups were supported by Iran and al-Qaeda in Iraq. The Iraq War caused at least one hundred thousand civilian deaths, as well as tens of thousands of military deaths The majority of deaths occurred as a result of the insurgency and civil conflicts between 2004 and 2007.

In 2007, the United States responded with a build-up of 170,000 troops which gave greater control to Iraq's government and military and was judged a success by many. In 2008, President Bush agreed to U.S. troop's withdrawal from Iraq. In December 2011, the U.S. troop's withdrawal was officially completed under President Barack Obama.

The Iraq War from 2013 to 2017, which is considered a domino effect of the invasion and occupation, caused at least 155,000 deaths, in addition to the displacement of more than 3.3 million people within the country.

In the summer of 2014, ISIL (Islamic State of Iraq)

launched a military offensive in northern Iraq and declared a worldwide Islamic caliphate, leading to Operation Inherent Resolve, another military response from the United States and its allies; and the United States became re-involved leading a new coalition and the insurgency. A 2019 U.S. Army study said Iran emerged as "the only victor" of the war.

The 2016 Chilcot Report, a British inquiry into the United Kingdom's decision to go to war concluded that *not every peaceful alternative had been examined*, that the U.K. and U.S. had undermined the United Nations Security Council in the process of declaring war, that the process of identification for a legal basis of war was "far from satisfactory," and that, taken together, the war was unnecessary. Kofi Annan called the invasion illegal under international law because it violated the UN Charter.

Operation Iraqi Freedom (the Iraq War) was a highly controversial invasion of a foreign country by the United States.

Consider the following:

- Saudis, not Iraqis, bombed the World Trade Center.

- U.S. invaded Iraq and killed hundreds of thousands of innocent Iraqis.
- Osama bin Laden was the master-mind of the World Trade Center bombing.
- U.S. assassinated bin Laden and family members in Afghanistan.
- U.S. militarily occupied Afghanistan a decade and a half after killing bin Laden.
- U.S. often killed innocent people with drone strikes in Afghanistan.

Afghanistan was harboring Osama bin Laden. After the September 11 attacks, U.S. President George W. Bush demanded that the Taliban hand over Osama bin Laden and expel al-Qaeda. Bin Laden had already been wanted by the FBI since 1998. The Taliban declined to extradite him and ignored demands to shut down terrorist bases and hand over other terrorist suspects apart from bin Laden.

On October 7, 2001, the U.S. launched Operation Enduring Freedom and with its close allies invaded Afghanistan toppling the Taliban government. The invasion's aims were to dismantle al-Qaeda, which had executed the September 11 attacks, and to deny it a safe base of operations in Afghanistan by removing the Taliban government from power.

On May 2, 2011, Osama bin Laden was killed by U.S special operations forces in Pakistan. The U.S. spent a decade fighting the Taliban, and then abruptly left.

In 2020, the U.S. left Afghanistan to the Taliban under an agreement ensuring a safe passage for American forces out of the country by mid-2021, but the U.S. retrograde from Afghanistan was ill-conceived, clumsy, embarrassing, and deadly. Even giving up the fight and leaving the battlefield turned out to be catastrophic.

U.S. troops were in Afghanistan due to George W. Bush's "War on Terror." ***The truth is that Saudi terrorists bombed the World Trade Center***, and the real reason that the U.S. attacked Iraq was because Saddam Hussein threatened Bush's father. There was no connection to Iraq and Afghanistan due to the so-called "War on Terror" because neither Iraq nor Afghanistan bombed the World Trade Center nor did they have weapons of mass destruction.

National laws forbade *"mercenary activity"* in the Western world, but U.S. mercenaries continued to flourish and thrive in the battlefields and cities of Iraq and Afghanistan. During the Iraq and Afghanistan excursions, "contractors," ex-military, law enforcement, and simply "wannabes," were paid outrageous salaries to be private security for corporations. They committed atrocities such as killing innocent civilians, and they were not subject to the Uniform Code of Military Justice (UCMJ).

The Vietnam War was not the only war with controversial issues, *the difference was that America turned against its own*—those who served in Vietnam. Biden's order for a quick withdrawal while not considering all of the consequences, left thousands of U.S. citizens and Afghans with U.S. or other visas stranded by the Taliban.

Biden eventually corrected his error in judgment and subsequent flights removed more personnel. The press reaction to Biden's overall handling of Afghanistan issues was conciliatory as opposed to the press accounts about Nixon and Vietnam. Nixon was vilified for being in a war he inherited; but Biden got a pass except for his disgraceful exit.

After Joe Biden became President, he changed the withdrawal date from May 1, 2021, to September 11, before moving it forward to August 31. After the original deadline had expired, and coinciding with the troop withdrawal, the Taliban launched a broad offensive and captured most of Afghanistan, finally taking

Kabul on August 15, 2021. The same day, the President of Afghanistan, Ashraf Ghani, fled the country and the Taliban declared victory ending the war. On August 16, Biden confirmed the Taliban takeover, and on August 30, the "last" American military plane departed Afghanistan, ending nearly 20 years of western military presence in the country.

Biden wanted to get out fast; but there was public uproar over the ill-conceived, quick U.S. extraction from Afghanistan that forced a troop and civilian evacuation eventually leaving the Taliban in charge. There is a saying that *Democrats begin wars and Republicans end them*, but in Afghanistan, George W. Bush, a Republican, started the war; and Biden, a Democrat, clumsily ended it.

Neither Bush nor Biden understood war. A swift withdrawal without thoroughly considering the relevant dynamics of doing so, as President Biden, a 5-time Vietnam deferment awardee, did, is a disastrous symbol and legacy of Afghanistan; and the invasion of a country for no legitimate reason, as Bush did in Iraq, is simply a war crime.

Hiram Johnson was a Republican politician from California who served in the U.S. Senate for 30 years, beginning in the midst of World War I and ending with his death in 1945 (the day the U.S. dropped its first atomic bomb on Hiroshima). He coined the phrase, *"The first casualty when war comes, is truth…."*

Comparisons of Afghanistan and Vietnam Wars

Julian Borger filed a report in Washington on November 4, 2021 about a Pentagon investigation finding that the U.S. drone strike in Kabul killing ten Afghan civilians was an "honest mistake;" hence, not requiring legal or disciplinary action. The report met widespread outrage from Congress and human rights groups. Critics said the report contributed to a culture of impunity and *failed to address systemic problems in the U.S. conduct of drone warfare, making future civilian casualties inevitable.* The victims of the August 29 drone strike included a worker for a U.S.-based aid organization and nine members of his family, including seven children.

The most reliable data, which was compiled by the New America Foundation, estimated that between 293 and 471 civilians were killed by drone strikes.

The U.S.A.F. Inspector General, Lt. Gen. Sami Said, found that the drone operators had confused a white

Toyota Corolla at the scene with a car linked to a terrorist group and also failed to see a child visible in surveillance footage two minutes before the strike. It further found no evidence of wrongdoing.

> *"The investigation found no violation of law, including the law of war. Execution errors combined with confirmation bias and communication breakdowns led to regrettable civilian casualties."*
>
> General Said told reporters at the Pentagon, *"It was an honest mistake, but it's not criminal conduct, random conduct, negligence."*

He noted that the high-pressure conditions surrounding the strike and fear of an imminent attack on Kabul airport by the Islamic State contributed to the mistake.

Perhaps the alleged "sins" or combat actions in the Vietnam War may be more understandable in light of what occurred in Afghanistan and Iraq.

After Joe Biden became President, he changed the withdrawal date from May 1, 2021, to September 11 before moving it forward to August 31. After the original deadline had expired, and coinciding with the troop withdrawal, the Taliban launched a broad offensive and captured most of Afghanistan, finally taking Kabul on August 15, 2021. On the same day, the President of Afghanistan, Ashraf Ghani, fled the country, and the Taliban declared victory ending the war.

Biden's order for a quick withdrawal, while not considering all of the consequences, left thousands of U.S. citizens and Afghans (who held U.S. or other visas) stranded by the Taliban. Biden eventually corrected his judgment error, and subsequent flights removed more personnel from Afghanistan.

On August 16, Biden confirmed the Taliban takeover, and on August 30, the "last" American military plane departed Afghanistan, ending nearly 20 years of western military presence in the country. Biden wanted to get out fast, but there was public uproar over the ill-conceived, quick U.S. extraction from Afghanistan that forced a troop and civilian evacuation that eventually left the Taliban in charge.

The press reaction to Biden's overall handling of Afghanistan issues was conciliatory as opposed to the press accounts about Nixon and Vietnam. Nixon was vilified for being in a war he inherited; Biden got a pass except for his disgraceful exit.

There is a saying that *Democrats begin wars and Republicans end wars*, but in Afghanistan, George W. Bush, a Republican, started the war; and Biden, a

Democrat, clumsily ended it. Neither Bush nor Biden understood war. A swift withdrawal without thoroughly considering the relevant dynamics, as President Biden (a 5-time Vietnam deferment awardee) did, is the disastrous legacy of Afghanistan.

Was Vietnam a Just War?

Vietnam Was a Just War

Over a half a century has passed since many served in Vietnam; and other wars, conflicts, actions, and the concepts of war evolved over time. *Vietnam was a "just war,"* but what is a "just war?" The following are synopsises of philosophical theories justifying warfare.

Just War Theory[1]

The Just War theory (jus belli justi), a doctrine or tradition of military ethics studied by military leaders, theologians, ethicists and policy makers, is to ensure that a war is ***morally justifiable through a series of criteria, all of which must be just***. The Just War theory is the belief that ***war with the right conduct is not always the worst option*** because important responsibilities, undesirable outcomes, or preventable atrocities may justify war. There are two groups of thought: "right to go to war" *(jus ad bellum)* and "right conduct in war" *(jus in bello)*.

---

1. Wikipedia. See credits for reference. Emphasis added.

The first group of criteria concerns the morality of going to war. The second group of criteria concerns the moral conduct within war. Opponents to the Just War theory state a stricter pacifist standard—there is never a justifiable basis for war, or they may condone a nationalist standard that a war only needs to serve a nation's interests to be justifiable.

Many philosophers think that one should not have a guilty conscience if he is required to fight. Other philosophers dignify the soldier's virtues while declaring their apprehensions for war, itself.

The "just war tradition" includes the historical rules or agreements applied to wars and the writings of various philosophers and lawyers throughout history.

Egypt

A 2017 study found that the Just War tradition can be traced as far back as to Ancient Egypt. Egyptian ethics of war usually centered on three main ideas, including the cosmological role of Egypt, the pharaoh as a divine office and executor of the will of the gods, and the superiority of the Egyptian state and population over all other states and peoples.

Egyptian political theology held that the pharaoh had the exclusive legitimacy to justly initiating a war, usually claimed to carry out the will of the gods. Pharaohs considered their sonship of the god Amun-Re as granting them absolute ability to declare war on the deity's behalf.

Pharaohs often visited temples prior to initiating campaigns, where the pharaoh was believed to receive their commands of war from the deities. As the period of the New Kingdom progressed and Egypt heightened its territorial ambition, so did the invocation of just war aid the justification of these efforts.

The universal principle of order and justice was central to the Egyptian notion of Just War and guaranteed that Egypt had no limits on what it could take, do, or use to guarantee the ambitions of the state.

Confucian

Chinese philosophy produced a massive body of work on warfare during the Warring States era. ***War was justified only as a last resort*** and only by the rightful sovereign and questioning the emperor's decision about the necessity of a military action was impermissible.

The success of a military campaign was sufficient proof that the campaign had been righteous.

Though Japan did not develop its own doctrine of Just War, between the 5th and 7th centuries they drew heavily from Chinese philosophy, especially from Confucius.

As part of the Japanese campaign taking the northeastern island Honshu, Japanese military portrayed their actions to "pacify" the Emishi people who were likened to "bandits" and "wild-hearted wolf cubs" and accused of invading Japan's frontier lands.

Ancient Greece and Rome

The notion of Just War in Europe originated and developed first in ancient Greece, and then in the Roman Empire. Aristotle first introduced the concept and terminology to the Hellenic world where war was a last resort and required conduct that would not make the restoration of peace impossible.

He believed that the ***cultivation of a military was necessary and good for the purpose of self-defense, not for conquering:***

> *"The proper object of practicing military training is not in order that men may enslave those who do not deserve slavery, but in order that first*

they may themselves avoid becoming enslaved to others."

In ancient Rome, a "just cause" for war might include the necessity of repelling an invasion, or retaliation for pillaging or a breach of a treaty. War was always potentially wrong and risked religious pollution and divine disfavor. A "Just War" *(bellum iustum)* required a ritualized declaration by the fetial priests.

Conventions of war and treaty-making were part of the *ius gentium*, the "law of nations," the customary moral obligations regarded as innate and universal to human beings.

Christian Views

Christian theory of a Just War began around the time of Augustine of Hippo. The Just War theory, with some amendments, is still used by Christians today as a guide to whether or not a war can be justified. ***War may be necessary and right, even though it may not be good.*** In the case of a country that has been invaded by an occupying force, war may be the only way to restore justice.

Saint Augustine believed individuals should not

resort immediately to violence, but ***God gave the sword to government for good reason.*** Augustine asserted that Christians, as part of a government, did not have to be ashamed of protecting peace and punishing wickedness when forced to do so by a government. He asserted that peacefulness in the face of a grave wrong that could only be stopped by violence would be a sin. Defense of one's self or others could be a necessity, especially when authorized by a legitimate authority.

Saint Thomas Aquinas held the Just War theory had a lasting impact on later generations and was part of an emerging consensus in Medieval Europe on Just War. In the 13th century, Aquinas, a Dominican friar, contemplated the teachings of the bible on peace and war in combination with ideas from Aristotle, Plato, Saint Augustine, and other philosophers whose writings were part of the Western canon reflecting in detail on peace and war.

In *Summa Theologica*, Aquinas asserted that it is not always a sin to wage war, and he set out criteria for a Just War. According to Aquinas, three requirements must be met: First, a rightful sovereign must command the war. Second, the war must be for just cause due to some wrong the attacked have committed. Thirdly, warriors must have the right intent to promote good and to avoid evil.

A Just War could be offensive, and injustice should not be tolerated to avoid war. Aquinas argued that on the battlefield, violence must only be used as a last resort. Soldiers needed to avoid cruelty and a Just War was limited by the conduct of just combatants.

Aquinas argued that it was only in the pursuit of justice, that the good intention of a moral act could justify negative consequences, including the killing of the innocent during a war.

Examples of Major Military Actions
Tet 1968

The Tet Offensive began at night, January 30 and 31. The first phase of the Tet Offensive ended by March 28, but fighting at Khe Sanh went into April. The NVA Tet Offensive ended on September 23 and was a failure. Most cities, with the notable exception of Hue, were liberated within a few days of the initial attack.

The Communist leadership in Hanoi gambled on a conventional assault they thought would sweep aside ARVN forces and topple the "puppet" government in Saigon, but NVA and VC advances were stopped by resilient ARVN defenders.

The widespread loss of life and destruction of property caused a decline in support for the Viet Cong among the South Vietnamese populace. ***U.S. and South Vietnamese officials declared that the Communists suffered a resounding military defeat,*** but Walter Cronkite claimed Tet was a Communist victory.

Battle of Hue

The Battle of Hue was the attack on the Imperial capital by forces of the North Vietnamese Army and South Vietnamese insurgents of the National Liberation Front during the Tet Offensive. A division-size force of North Vietnamese Army and Viet Cong soldiers launched a well-coordinated multi-pronged attack on the city.

Their strategic objective was to "liberate" the entire city, but it failed totally as its occupants were solidly on the side of the American and South Vietnamese. With a wartime population of about 140,000 persons, Hue retained much of its pre-war ambiance. It had been immune to much of the war.

Unknown to the allies, enemy regiments were on the move toward Hue. The 6th NVA had as its three primary objectives—the Mang Ca headquarters compound, the Tay Loc Airfield, and the Imperial Palace, all in the Citadel. The 4th NVA was to attack the modern city south of the Perfume River.

The Communist forces hoped a popular uprising by the "oppressed" people in South Vietnam would lead to a general uprising and overthrow of the "puppet" regime supported by the United States. Hue was the only city completely occupied by the Communist forces during the massive offensive and was the scene of violent and close-quarter fighting that raged for a month, from January 31 to February 25, 1968.

The 26-day effort by the U.S. Marines, U.S. Army, and ARVN to recapture the Citadel produced a stunning military defeat for the Communists. Ironically, the strategic U.S. victory during Tet went to the Communists. The scenes of bloody fighting on TV in Hue, Saigon, and other cities in Vietnam so shocked the American people that the pressure to withdraw from the war was overwhelming.

Vietnam was the first-ever American televised war with nightly news coverage; people watched the blood and napalm as they ate their dinner. The draft in America was immensely unpopular, with many college-age men burning their draft cards, heading to Canada, or claiming to be a drug addict or homosexual to get out of serving.

The Battle of Hue and the Tet Offensive of 1968 turned many Americans against the war; Walter Cronkite, the most trusted man in America, did, too.

The NVA attack began early on January 31, and by 0800, North Vietnamese troops raised the red and blue Viet Cong banner with its gold star over the Citadel flag tower. It was quite a shock to the allies. The U.S. Marines engaged in a house-to-house, booby-trap-infested ordeal as they swept through every inch of the city. The monsoon season made it impossible for U.S. forces to use air support. Armor and airstrikes were extremely limited due to the conditions, and to lessen casualties, the Allied forces were ordered not to bomb or shell the city for fear of destroying the historic structures.

As the intensity of the battle increased, the policy was eliminated. The Communist forces constantly used snipers hidden inside buildings or in small holes,

After the recapture of Hue in 1968, several mass graves were discovered. Many had been clubbed, shot, or simply buried alive. As many as 2,800 South Vietnamese civilians were executed.

and prepared makeshift machine-gun bunkers. On February 24, the U.S. Marines finally prevailed and had retaken the Citadel and NVA flag.

The Communists suffered heavy losses in this battle, losing 5,133 men at Hue; about 3,000 more were estimated to be killed outside of the city. The whole attack force was wiped out. Approximately 2,800 people were killed by the NVA and VC simply because they were pro-allies. Mass graves of executed and other atrocities were unearthed. There were 142 American losses.

An interesting and little-mentioned aspect of the Battle of Hue was the use of fire team assault boats by the Marines. A fire team assault boat platoon consisted of 12 boats. Each boat was 16 feet long, made of fiberglass, had a 50 hp Mercury motor, four men, and a mounted M-60 machine gun. These assault boats conducted river operations—patrolling the waterways and acting as waterborne infantry at the heavily defended East Gate of the Citadel, transporting wounded across the Perfume River, and conducting search and destroy missions.

Marines' tanks and ARVNs traversed a wall, captured the east gate, and were moving toward the city, when the they were ordered not to take it for political reasons because ARVNs were to take back the city of

Hue. So, ARVNs, not the Marines who captured the east gate, entered Hue first. Politics of war.

Battle of Firebase Ripcord

The Battle of Fire Support Base Ripcord was a four-month long battle from March 12 to July 23, 1970 between elements of the U.S. Army 101st Airborne Division and two reinforced NVA divisions. Attempting to retake the initiative, the 101st was to rebuild the abandoned Fire Support Base Ripcord in the A Shau Valley. They relied heavily on helicopters in the difficult terrain as the 101st became an air assault division. The firebase was set on four hilltops as outposts for a planned offensive by the Marines to search and destroy the NVA supply lines in the mountains overlooking the A Shau valley. As the 101st soldiers rebuilt the base and prepared the attack on the enemy supply lines, the NVA launched sporadic attacks from March 12 until June 30. An estimated 25,000 NVA troops were positioned in the A Shau Valley area at the time.

On the morning of July 1, 1970, the NVA started firing mortars and besieged the firebase for 23 days; 75 U.S. servicemen were killed. The battle for the hilltops raged for days. Surrounded and outnumbered almost ten to one and running low on supplies, the 101st held out and kept the enemy from overrunning the firebase. It was the last major confrontation between U.S. ground forces and North Vietnam in the war. The final death toll was 138 American soldiers and 3 men missing in action.

1972 Spring-Summer Offensive

The 1972 Spring-Summer Offensive or the Easter Offensive, was conducted by the NVA against the ARVN and the United States military between March 30 and October 22, 1972. The U.S. high command expected an attack in 1972, but the size and ferocity of the assault stunned the defenders because the attackers struck on three fronts simultaneously, with the bulk of the NVA.

This first attempt by the NVA to invade the south since Tet, 1968, was characterized by conventional infantry-armor assaults backed by heavy artillery with both sides using the latest technological advances in weapons systems. The NVA major offensive in the South on March 30 included 40,000 NVA troops and over 600 armored vehicles and tanks crossing the border from the North and Cambodia. It was the largest offensive operation since 300,000 Chinese troops had

U.S. Army Airborne soldiers move through Viet Cong sniper fire toward the jungle after being dropped by Hueys in a rice field.

crossed the Yalu River into North Korea during that war. The Communists seized the cities of Quang Tri, Hue, An Loc, and Kon Tum.

The U.S. responded by carpet bombing the North; though South Vietnam recaptured Quang Tri, it lost 10% of its land to the North. The fighting ended on October 22. Although North Vietnam was repelled, they still kept their newly occupied territory and got their bargaining chip.

In the I Corps Tactical Zone, NVA forces overran South Vietnamese defensive positions in a month-long battle and captured the city of Quang Tri before attempting to seize Hue. NVA similarly eliminated frontier defense forces in the II Corps Tactical Zone and seized the provincial capital of Kon Tum, threatening to open a way to the sea, which would have split South Vietnam in two.

Northeast of Saigon, in the III Corps Tactical Zone, NVA forces overran Loc Ninh and advanced to assault the capital of Bình Long Province at An Loc. The campaign was in three phases: April was a month of NVA advances; May became a period of equilibrium; in June and July the ARVN counterattacked, recapturing Quang Tri City in September. Initial North Vietnamese successes were hampered by high casualties, inept tactics, and the increasing application of U.S. and South Vietnamese air power.

The offensive was not designed to win the war outright but to gain as much territory and destroy as many units of the ARVN as possible and to improve the North's negotiating position as the Paris Peace Accords were concluding.

A result of the offensive was the U.S. launching Operation Linebacker II, the first sustained bombing of North Vietnam by the U.S. since November 1968. The ARVN troops fought bravely and repulsed and drove the NVA back.

The Vietnamization proved successful. Nixon did not send in U.S. ground troops during the invasion, and he continued the final withdraw of the last U.S. combat troops that year.

Despite post-war characterizations, the ARVN troops proved they could stand up to the NVA. The combination of bombing the rail lines in the North, the mining of harbors, and the "December bombing" campaign put North Vietnam at a severe disadvantage.

Although ARVN (South Vietnamese forces) withstood their greatest trial thus far in the conflict, the NVA gained valuable territory within South Vietnam from which to launch future offensives and obtained a better bargaining position at the peace negotiations being conducted in Paris.

Paris Peace Accords

As leaders were surprised when the U.S. halted the bombing campaign in January, they later admitted being at their breaking point. Nixon knew the new Congress would not support his war efforts, and he wanted a deal before they were to take office. The 1972 Easter Offensive prompted Nixon to bomb Haiphong and Hanoi and end U.S. action in the war. South Vietnam was forced to agree to a deal they did not like only to appease both the President and Congress. President Nixon was adamant about getting his "peace with honor."

On January 27, 1973, the Paris Peace Accords ended the Vietnam War and specified that U.S. forces and Communist forces were to leave South Vietnam immediately, but the U.S. could send war material to South Vietnam if the NVA and VC renewed hostilities. U.S. POWs would be returned, and U.S. forces left Vietnam (except for the Embassy) in accordance with the Paris Peace Accords.

Before U.S. forces left Vietnam in 1973, thousands

of South Vietnamese sought refuge elsewhere and left Vietnam as the "boat people," but the ARVN (South Vietnamese) had developed into a force that could defend itself if the U.S. continued supplying arms and equipment.

After U.S. forces exited, the North Vietnamese Army and Viet Cong renewed invading cities in South Vietnam in violation of the Peace Accords.

In June 1973, the Case-Church Amendment, prohibited further U.S. military activity in Vietnam, unless the president got Congressional approval in advance. Congress stopped support of war materials to South Vietnamese forces as the NVA resumed attacks. In the end, Congress refused to fund the war material for the South Vietnamese who desperately needed it.

The Case-Church Amendment sealed the fate of South Vietnam and the entire region. Although most units fought valiantly, South Vietnamese forces ran out of ammo, fuel, and equipment to fight as the NVA intensified its invasion of South Vietnam.

On April 9, 1975, the Communists entered Dong Nai Province, the final swath which led to Saigon. In 1974, the Watergate issue forced Nixon to resign.

In April 1975, two years after U.S. forces left, NVA and VC troops captured Saigon. The antiwar crowd rejoiced as NVA tanks entered the Saigon palace grounds. The U.S. military tried to save South Vietnam who were betrayed by their own people.

Battle of Xuan Loc

The Battle of Xuan Loc was unique for the Vietnam War. It involved division-size units, devastatingly effective Viet Nam Air Force (VNAF) airpower, and sophisticated U.S.-made Daisy Cutter Bombs. It was the last major battle of the Vietnam War. From the beginning of 1975, the NVA forces swept through the northern provinces of South Vietnam unopposed. The ARVN devoted almost all of their remaining mobile forces, especially the *18th Division, under Brigadier General Le Minh Dao*, to the defense of the strategic crossroads town of Xuan Loc, hoping to stall the NVA advance.

The 18th Division lodged themselves in the town of Xuan Loc and were able to block North Vietnam's advance for two weeks. The ARVN held Xuan Loc and counterattacked and fought against impossible odds. It was described as "heroic and gallant" by the South Vietnamese defenders and as one of the few places where the RVN, though outnumbered, stood and fought with a tenacity which stunning their oppo-

Brigadier General Lê Minh Đảo

nents. The stand of the ARVN so impressed the rest of the entire South Vietnamese Army who previously routed, that they grew confident again.

The steel defensive line at Xuan Loc (Long Khanh) held firm after twelve days and nights of ferocious combat against the North Vietnamese Communist forces. The fighting was harsh and severe, but the ARVN troops held up the assault on Saigon for two weeks. Xuan Loc was reduced to rubble in the fight, and its population fled in a mass exodus.

The NVA 4th Corps forces, which engaged in the battle, had suffered heavy losses; therefore, the Headquarters of the Ho Chi Minh Campaign hastily changed their plan for the attack on Saigon and abandoned its efforts against Xuan Loc and became a "reserve force." The forces of the North Vietnamese 3rd Corps in Tay Ninh and 2nd Corps at the Nuoc Trong base would be used to make the "major effort" to attack and capture Saigon.

Xuan Loc was no longer a "hot point," and the Headquarters of ARVN 3rd Corps/Military Region 3 ordered the 18th Infantry Division and all units participating in the Xuan Loc (Long Khanh) battle to retreat to Bien Hoa on April 20, 1975, to establish a new line defending the outer approaches to Saigon.

This withdrawal marked the end of Thieu's political career, as he resigned on April 21. After Xuan Loc fell on April 21, the NVA battled with the last remaining elements (III Corps Armored Task Force, remnants of the 18th Infantry Division, and depleted Marine, Airborne, and Ranger Battalions) in a fighting retreat that lasted nine days until they reached Saigon.

The North Vietnamese broke through Xuan Loc with Soviet T54 tanks and headed straight toward Bien Hoa, arriving at Saigon at the end of the month.

South Vietnam fought bravely as long as it could until the U.S. Congress cut off funding for weapons and supplies, which the U.S. had previously promised.

At a dinner in Phoenix honoring Vietnam veterans, I met General Le Minh Dao who spent 17 years in Communist "re-education camps" after the war. He was first sent to a camp in northern Vietnam, where he spent 12 years, before being transferred to the south for another five years.

After his release in May 1992, he received political asylum in the United States and settled there in April 1993. He was a humble, kind man and still greatly appreciative of the U.S. support for his country in the Vietnam War. He was a true warrior and patriot, and I was honored to meet him.

The Army of the Republic of Vietnam

Communist sympathizers and the antiwar movement often demeaned the Army of the Republic of Vietnam (ARVN), the ground forces of the South Vietnamese military, which had an estimated 1,394,000 casualties (killed and wounded) during the Vietnam War.

The ARVN began as a postcolonial army that was trained by and closely affiliated with the United States. It changed from a "blocking-force" to a modern conventional force using helicopter deployment in combat. ARVN played a defensive role with an incomplete modernization during the American intervention. After Vietnamization, it expanded, up-geared, and reorganized its military to assume the role of the departing American forces.

By 1974, ARVN became a much more effective military force. Robert Thompson, a counterinsurgency expert and Nixon adviser, noted that ARVN Regular Forces were very well-trained and second only to the American and Israeli forces in the Free World. General Creighton Abrams said that 70% of units were on par with the U.S. Army.

At ARVN's peak, an estimated one in nine citizens of South Vietnam were enlisted. It was the world's fourth-largest army composed of Regular Forces and many voluntary Regional and Village-level militias. It was a dual military-civilian administrative entity competing with the VC as it still had issues of political loyalty appointments, corruption in leadership, factional infighting, and sometimes open internal conflict.

After Saigon fell to the NVA, the ARVN were dissolved; some high-ranking officers fled the country to the U.S. or elsewhere. Thousands of former ARVN officers were sent to re-education camps by the Communist government.

Vietnamization allowed ARVN forces to take over the fighting after the Americans withdrew, but the U.S. Congress did not honor the terms of the Paris Peace Accords promising to replace military equipment for the Vietnamese forces who depended on U.S. equipment.

Five ARVN generals committed suicide to avoid capture by the NVA/VC. Military and civilians braved the ocean, sharks, and pirates seeking safety from the North Vietnamese Army. It was a tragic ending for the South Vietnamese.

President Nixon's power was diminished by the Watergate scandal dogging him and Congress' ending financial military aid to South Vietnam.

The Fall of Saigon

On April 9, 1975, NVA entered Dong Nai Province, the final swath that led to Saigon. Thousands of South Vietnamese sought refuge elsewhere and left Vietnam as the "boat people." When Xuan Loc fell on April 21, all order collapsed. Hoping to find safety in American-held Saigon, the ARVN and South Vietnam civilians made a chaotic retreat from the advancing North Vietnamese. Xuan Loc was only 26 miles away from Saigon, so the Communists were already at their doorstep. By April 27, 1975, Saigon was surrounded. On April 29, the shelling began, and on April 30, the NVA entered the capital.

The orderly evacuation of Americans and South Vietnam civilians became chaotic as NVA armored columns crashed through the gates of South Vietnam's Presidential Palace. U.S. military involvement in the Vietnam War finally ended on April 30, 1975.

Ultimately, estimates of the number of Vietnamese soldiers and civilians killed vary from 966,000 to 3,812,000. Current 2017 records report that the conflict resulted in 58,318 U.S. fatalities—then there were the "boat people" and the "reeducation camps."

Mayaguez Incident

On May 12, 1975, Cambodian Navy gunboats seized the American merchant ship, *SS Mayaguez*, in international waters off Cambodia's coast. The ship was being towed toward the Cambodian mainland when word reached the White House. President Ford was adamant that this would not be allowed to deteriorate into another drawn-out *Pueblo* incident. He wanted to dispel a perception among U.S. friends and adversaries that America was "a helpless giant" and an erratic ally lacking determination.

The U.S. response to the seizure would be a military operation executed by an *ad hoc* force of airmen, Marines, and sailors. The U.S. had no diplomatic relations with the Khmer Rouge, which had taken control of Cambodia in previous weeks; nearby U.S. forces stationed in Thailand were numerically insufficient for ground action against Cambodia, and no U.S. warships were in the district. Time was a compelling factor as the big concern was that the Cambodians would transfer the crew to the mainland, making the rescue operation more arduous.

Multiple plans were considered. According to then Chief of Staff General David C. Jones, five plans were prepared. Option Four, a twin-pronged marine assault coupled with the bombing of selected targets, was Ford's choice.

In such situations as hostage rescue attempts, planning is usually based on assumptions or speculation, especially during the first hours or days of the crisis. Intelligence data were sufficient for an operation with all its possibilities. Within a few minutes of receiving the mayday message sent by the *Mayaguez*, a Ready Alert Bird was airborne. By 10:30 p m , the first report on the *Mayaguez* was received at Cubi Point Naval Air Station. It was too dark for Ready Alert Bird and its crew to eyeball the ship, but they could see a captured merchant vessel on their radar screens as a big image flanked by two little images.

Option Four was an extravagant scheme that employed two destroyers, one aircraft carrier, two Marine units with twelve helicopters, and a generous complement of Air Force fighters, bombers, and reconnaissance aircraft were selected. Ford ordered the aircraft carrier *Coral Sea* and other navy ships to proceed at full speed to the Gulf of Thailand, as well as planes in the Philippines to locate the *Mayaguez* and keep it in view. A Navy P-3 located the ship anchored off Koh-Tang Island, 40 miles from Cambodia. Several observance aircraft were damaged by gunfire from the island.

A battalion-sized Marine rescue team was airlifted from Okinawa to U-Tapao Airforce Base in the Gulf of Thailand, about three hundred miles from Koh-Tang. The destroyer *USS Holt* was directed to seize the *Mayaguez*, while Marines, airlifted and supported by the Air Force, would rescue the crew, at least some of whom were believed to be held on Koh-Tang. Concurrently, the *Coral Sea* would launch four bombing strikes on military targets near Kompong Som to convince the Khmer Rouge that the U.S. was serious.

Expecting only light resistance, the U.S. troops were met by a force of 150 to 200 heavily armed Khmer Rouge soldiers who shot down three of the first eight helicopters and damaged two others. About one hundred Marines were put ashore, but it became clear that substantial reinforcements would be needed. The assault force was supported by Air Force planes, but the attack was not going well.

While the firefight on Koh-Tang was intense, bombing targets on the mainland convinced the Khmer Rouge leaders that they had underestimated U.S. resolve. A fishing boat approached the destroyer *Wilson* with white flags flying, and the 39 crewmen of the *Mayaguez* were aboard.

The Marines on Koh-Tang were ordered to disengage and withdraw, but Khmer Rouge troops continued the battle, taking the offensive. Air Force helicopters moved through heavy fire to withdraw U.S. forces. The last of 230 Marines were not evacuated until after dark on the night of May 15.

As they had throughout the Vietnam War, helicopter crews performed with unsurpassed heroism. Eighteen Marines and airmen were killed or missing in the assault and withdrawal from Koh-Tang. Twenty-three others were killed in a helicopter crash in route from Nakhon Phanom to U-Tapao, but the objectives of the operation were achieved. The *Mayaguez* and its crew had been rescued, though at high cost.

History of Air Cavalry

Horses to Helicopters

In ancient warfare, as weapons developed through the ages, so did the modes of transportation. Oxen, horses, carts, wagons, chariots, and horse cavalry influenced the success of armies and the rise and fall of civilizations and nations.

The reasons for the use of horses were similar to the reasons for the use of helicopters in Vietnam—mobility. *Mobility* is one of the main principles in conducting warfare. Horses could take a fighting person from point A to point B quickly to influence the battle. The origin of the use of the horse as a means of transport goes back to prehistoric times. Man has progressed from riding a horse to riding spacecraft.

Consider "centaurs"—mythological beings part man and part horse which probably originated with pastoral peoples living on horseback. Some researchers think horseback riding evolved in the Eurasian steppes and mountains above the Mesopotamian plain.

Rise of the horse eras:

- Era of Consumption (50,000BC to present). Man hunted and ate horses.

- Era of Utilization and Status (4000BC to 1900AD). Man learned to use the horse.

- Era of Herding (3500BC to present). Man raised horses.

- Era of the Chariot (1700BC-400AD). Man had limited use of the horse in war.

- Era of the Cavalry (700BC – 1942AD). Man had horse-mounted units in war.

- Era of Agriculture (900AD – 1945AD). Man used "horsepower" to farm.

- Era of the Carriage (1700AD-1920AD). Man used horse for carriage transportation.

- Era of Leisure – (1900 to present). Man uses horse for recreation.

From ancient times, man had 6,000 years of history with the horse and its speed and power allowing man to travel faster and farther than on foot. The horse transformed the world and gave war enhanced mobility.

Archaeological discoveries in India, Persia, Assyria, and Egypt show prehistoric man domesticated the horse in the polished stone age. A Chinese military code dating from the reign of the emperor Hoang-Ti, 2637 B.C., placed the cavalry on the wings of the army.

A 2500 B.C. Sumerian illustration of warfare depicts an equine pulling wagons.

By 1600 B.C., the improved harness and chariot designs made chariot warfare common throughout the Ancient Near East.

By 1400 B.C., the use of smelted iron to make weapons gave the infantry supremacy, but around 1350 B.C. the earliest written training manual for war horses was written as a guide for training chariot horses.

In the 300s B.C., King Phillip II of Macedonia used cavalry as major military units for the first time in Europe. By 360 B.C. formal cavalry tactics replaced the chariot, and new training methods were devised. The Greek cavalry officer, Xenophon, wrote an extensive treatise on horsemanship. The saddle, stirrup, and later, the horse collar—all revolutionized the horse's effectiveness in battle.

The Hebrews understood the use of the horse in

war (Job 39:18-25 KJV) as did the Persians (Cyrus at the battle of Thymbra) and the Greeks and Romans. The Greeks were especially skilled horsemen using no stirrup but had both bridle and bit and rode bareback, or on a cloth or skin, strapped to the horse.

A feature of their games was performing feats on horseback.

Nomad tribes in Asia were the first to use cavalry for scouting and pursuit of a routed enemy. Cavalry units were a leading part of the Roman army in the late 300s A.D. The horse's mobility changed warfare and civilizations. In the East both saddles and stirrups had been used since the 1st century, and European feudalism was made possible by the introduction of saddles in the 4th century, and stirrups in the 8th century in the West. During the middle-ages, only knights and their squires fought on horseback.

Cavalry dominated local wars in Europe and the attempts to fend off Norsemen, Magar, and Muslim raiders. The Crusades were essentially cavalry wars and sieges which were eventually won by the Muslims. Oliver Cromwell created the Cavalry Charge.

"Chivalry" has the same origin as our modern words cavalier and cavalry. The word *"Cavalry"* comes from the French word *cavalerie*, or *chevalerie* and the Latin

word *caballus*, meaning "horse." Chivalry simply means "service on horseback" and was the system, spirit, or customs, and the idealized code of gallantry, honor, and virtues of piety, honor, valor, courtesy, chastity and loyalty of medieval knighthood.

In the 13th century, the Mongols amazing military success was based on cavalry. In Europe, infantry remained dominant until the threat of light cavalry relying on archery, typified by the Mongols, brought about the adoption of heavy-armored cavalry, developed first by the Parthian Empire (ancient Iran). As the Middle Ages ended, infantry came to the fore again, but cavalry remained prominent in the armies of Louis XIV, Frederick II (Frederick the Great) and Napoleon.

During Medieval times, two distinctions of cavalry emerged—heavy and light cavalry. Heavy cavalry referred to those heavily armored knights used as shock troops charging the enemy with lances, often in close formation, similar to the shoulder-to-shoulder tactics of infantry charges in 19th century American armies. Armored knights charging at full gallop was spectacular and overwhelming to the enemy.

Light cavalry carried less armor and were a reconnaissance force for scouting, screening, and skirmishing.

The 19th-century cavalry was frequently used by Europeans in colonial wars, by the U.S. Army and plains people in the Indian Wars, and in the U.S. Civil War. The movie images of the Cavalry charges on the western frontier are iconic.

European light cavalry was largely equipped and armed with sabers, carbines, and pistols and focused on wide-ranging reconnaissance and security tasks. In the mid-1800s, U.S. Cavalry used small arms (pistols and carbines) and *dismounted their horses* to fight with the enemy. A century later, Air Cavalry soldiers in Vietnam used small arms (pistols and carbines) and *dismounted their helicopters* to fight with the enemy.

By the 1700s, heavy cavalry were still shock troops, and light cavalry were still reconnaissance—scouting, screening, and skirmishing. In the U.S., four regiments of light dragoons and other mounted forces fought in the Revolutionary War.

Dragoons were elite mounted troops trained to fight on horseback and on foot. The term *"dragoon"* came from the nickname for their weapon, the carbine or short musket, called "the dragon," referring to the fire that emitted from the gun when fired; hence, the term "dragon" or "dragoon soldiers." Dragoons fought in the War of 1812, but by 1815, all mounted forces were disbanded.

In 1832, a battalion of mounted rangers was organized but soon disbanded. In 1833, the First Regiment of Dragoons was organized, and there were no other mounted forces in the United States Army.

In 1844, the American Army consisted of 8573 men; the ten companies of the First Dragoons had about 623 men. After the first five companies were recruited, they were sent to Fort Gibson to winter. The others followed later. Each company at full strength had a captain, a first lieutenant, a second lieutenant, four sergeants, four corporals, two buglers, one farrier and blacksmith, and fifty privates.

The men were armed with Hall's carbines and later with musketoons, dragoon sabers called "old wrist-breakers" of the Prussian pattern, and horse pistols. All of the weapons had drawbacks. The carbine, carried muzzle down, lost the charge from the chamber and could not stand much wear. Sabers were a nuisance in Indian fighting as they jingled and were difficult to keep sharp.

One of the differences between the dragoons and the cavalry was that dragoons rode horses for mobility and usually dismounted when they went into action to fight as infantry using carbines, musketoons, or pistols. They also had sabers and could fight mounted or dismounted. Cavalry fought almost exclusively on horseback. Air Cavalry was transported by helicopters but fought almost exclusively dismounted.

In 1845, the U.S. Army organized a regiment of mounted riflemen for defense of forts along the Oregon Trail. They had no sabers, but they had rifles. The regiment fought in the U.S.-Mexican War and was later assigned duties in the far West. From 1852-1853, two companies were stationed at Fort Scott which the Army abandoned in 1853. In 1855, the U.S. Army organized two cavalry regiments mounted on horseback which were more of a reconnaissance or screening force.

By the late 1850s, cavalry, dragoons, and mounted riflemen were in the Army—two regiments of dragoons, one regiment of mounted riflemen, and two regiments of light cavalry. In 1861, the army redesignated mounted regiments as cavalry ending the era of the dragoon.

During WW I, due to trench warfare, horsemen were used only in small numbers on the plains of Eastern Europe and in the Middle East; but they were decisive in the Arab revolt.

In WW II, the Russian Cassocks and the German Uhlan Cavalries are considered to be among the world's greatest cavalry as were the Polish and Soviet armies employed against Germany. Many believed the Russians had used 300,000 horse cavalrymen, but the highly mobile tank and armored units ended the use of mounted troops. As the horse, motor cars, tanks, armored personnel carriers, and other vehicles revolutionized the concept of warfare, so did the helicopter.

Air Cavalry in Vietnam

Air Cavalry in Vietnam was *infantry mounted on helicopters for mobility* to conduct missions. Today, helicopters are everywhere (e.g., law enforcement, search and rescue, land survey, mineral exploration, medical evacuation, etc.); and they are key to modern military operations (e.g., troop transport, medical transport, logistics transport, reconnaissance, fire support, etc.). But when and how did it all begin?

In 1962, the need for a new type of unit became apparent to the Tactical Mobility Requirements Board (normally referred to as the Howze Board) of the U.S. Army. Most of the military hierarchy focused primarily on the Soviet threat to Western Europe, perceived the threat as requiring heavy, conventional units; thus, the creation of new, light airmobile units could only occur at the expense of heavier units.

Despite the challenge, the Howze board studied the application of Army aircraft to the traditional cavalry role of mounted combat especially in reconnaissance, security, and target requisition. It also studied possible Army operations in Southeast Asia, Europe, Northeast Asia, and the Middle East.

One of the board's most innovative concepts proposed an *Air Cavalry Combat Brigade (ACCB) to fight from an aerial mounted position performing the historical role of cavalry in exploitation, pursuit, counterattack, delay, and flank protection.* This brigade was designed for offense to seek out and destroy the enemy while doing traditional cavalry missions. The board considered a Combined Arms Air Brigade to give command a decisive combat unit.

At the same time, the incoming Kennedy administration was placing a much greater emphasis on the need to fight "small wars," or counter-insurgencies, and was strongly supportive of officers such as General Howze who were embracing new technologies. The Board commissioned tests for a new kind of unit. On February 11, 1963, the new experimental unit, the 11th Air Assault Division, was formed at Fort Benning, Georgia, combining light infantry with integral helicopter transport and air support. Some wanted to keep conventional warfare development, but the Secretary of Defense, Robert McNamara, pushed through the changes in 1965 to get Pentagon support for a counter-insurgency doctrine.

Events in Vietnam sped up the decision to convert the 11th Air Assault (Test) to a combat division. Support from the newly appointed senior Army commanders, including the new Chief of Staff, General Wheeler, helped to drive through the changes. The 11th Air Assault Division assets were merged with the co-located 2nd Infantry Division and reflagged as the 1st Cavalry Division (Airmobile), continuing the tradition of the 1st Cavalry Division.

On July 1, 1965, the 1st Cavalry Division (Airmobile) was activated and was composed of the resources of the 11th Air Assault Division (Test), the 10th Air Transport Brigade, and the 2nd Infantry Division. Within several months, in August and September, the ***1st Cavalry Division (Airmobile) was the first full U.S. Army division deployed to Vietnam***. Air mobility became intertwined with the challenges of Vietnam and its varied terrain—jungles, rivers, and mountains, which complicated ground movement.

When the 1st Air Cavalry Division arrived in Qui Nhon in 1965, it brought U.S. troop strength to 125,000 and was a true "air mobile" division of specialized light infantry trained, organized, and equipped specifically to perform complex, rapid, and dynamic tasks in air assault operations. Helicopters, instead of horses and tanks, increased maneuver of soldiers into battle in Vietnam and into the future.

Army FM 3-0:

> "Maneuver–Place the enemy in a position of disadvantage through The flexible application of combat power. Maneuver is the movement of forces in relation to the enemy to gain positional advantage. Effective maneuver keeps the enemy off balance and protects the force. It is used to exploit successes, to preserve freedom of action, and to reduce vulnerability. It continually poses new problems for the enemy by rendering his actions ineffective, eventually leading to defeat."

The "1st Air Cav" started it all performing traditional "cavalry" tactics—raids, search and destroy, flanking, screening, blocking, reconnaissance, and combat air assaults using helicopters as their "horses" riding into battle and dismounting to fight as Dragoons used to do. The 1st Cav troops were like "Dragoons" (mounted infantry), but maybe "Air Dragoon" was just not as sexy a name as "Air Cavalry."

Helicopters transported light infantry soldiers to

landing zones "prepped" by artillery fire to suppress the enemy. After the gunships rocketed and machine-gunned the landing zone, soldiers dismounted the helicopters and conducted search and destroy operations. *The Air Cavalry had missions that compared to those of the horse cavalry* because Air Cavalry had significant maneuverability and the advantage over infantry to do long-range reconnaissance, security missions, and to maneuver and concentrate forces for decisive actions by:

- Close reconnaissance to detect enemy weaknesses
- Flank and rear security of the infantry line
- Countering enemy cavalry
- Counterattacking enemy infantry attacks
- Reserves
- Administering the decisive blow to a faltering enemy
- Covering retreat
- Pursuing a retreating enemy.

History of Air Mobility

The first Army "airmobile" division (1st Cavalry Division-Airmobile) was structured with its own organic aviation and was the first full airmobile division sent to Vietnam in 1965. It served until the war's end in 1973 excelling in the traditional cavalry missions to reconnoiter, screen, delay, and conduct raids over wide terrain with helicopters.

It was perfect for fighting the war in Vietnam (RVN)—quick deployment of air mobile (helicopter transported) troops supported by helicopter gunships in varied terrain like jungle clearings, rice paddies, mountains, and sandy terrain along the coast, to find and engage the enemy. For its overall service, the 1st Cavalry Division (Airmobile) was awarded the Presidential Unit Citation; and its soldiers earned 25 Medals of Honor, 120 Distinguished Service Crosses, 2,766 Silver Stars, 2,697 Distinguished Flying Crosses, and 8,408 Bronze Stars for Valor.

The "First Team" was the only American division to fight in all four corps' tactical zones. The bulk of the division began departing Vietnam in late April 1970, while the 3rd Brigade remained until June 1972; the last air cavalry troops departing Vietnam in early 1973.

Airmobile operations would take on a new dimension and be replaced with emphasis on anti-armor tactics in the Middle East and to protect Europe. In 1973, General Abrams took over from General Westmoreland and implemented a pacification strategy rather than Westmoreland's attrition strategy. Nixon continued the extensive bombing of North Vietnam and forced the end of the war.

The war ended as the parties signed the Peace Accords in 1973 with the proviso that if the Communists violated the treaty, the U.S. would resupply South Vietnam with war material.

The progression from Air Cavalry to Air Assault to Night Stalkers began in 1965 when the 1st Cavalry Division (Airmobile) was the first division to conduct helicopter airmobile missions in Vietnam. In mid-1968, the 101st Airborne Division also became an "airmobile" division. The Vietnam War ended for the U.S. in 1973, with 1st Cavalry troops being the last combat units to leave Vietnam.

Vietnam Was A Just War

In October 1974, the 101st Airborne Division (Airmobile), dropped its title of "airmobile" in favor of "air assault" integrating attack, transport, and observation aircraft with fighting elements of the division. It became the 101st Air Assault Division.

The 1976 edition of FM 100-5, *Operations*, emphasized the post-Vietnam War thinking to reduce airmobile capabilities of active defense; instead, it emphasized airpower—close air support and anti-armor roles to meet the anticipated threats (e.g., Germany, Soviet armored divisions, Fulda Gap, later, Iraq).

Army doctrine of high, mid, and low-intensity conflict levels changed by late FY 1989 to operational continuum which defined various strategic environments, characterized as (1) peacetime competition, (2) conflict, or (3) war. This Army jargon simply characterized the evolution of perceived types of warfare.

"Peacetime competition" was disaster relief, joint training exercises, nation-building, peacekeeping, counterdrug operations, and military show of force. "Conflict" was counter-terrorism, contingency operations, insurgency and counter-insurgency situations. "War" was a sustained armed conflict at the strategic, operational, and tactical levels.

In April 1980, the Operation Eagle Claw attempt to rescue American hostages in Tehran, Iran failed. In August 1980, the 1st Air Cavalry was transformed into a heavy armored division focusing on AirLand Battle, and it was no longer a ready-reaction heliborne force as it was in Vietnam.

The Army reorganized the 1st Air Cavalry for a perceived "threat" of Soviet Army's armored and mechanized-infantry divisions in Europe. Apache helicopters armed with anti-tank Hell-fire missiles were the "school solution" in the Army's Command and General Staff course.

In 1984, the doctrine of AirLand Battle became the primary battle plan of U.S. NATO forces as it extensively studied the new "threat" of Soviet Army armored and mechanized divisions, and military operations changed. The handwriting was on the wall—there would be no more "airmobile" units transporting large airmobile infantry in the new Army. The iconic image of Air Cavalry troops of Vietnam fame was history.

President Jimmy Carter ordered the former Chief of Naval Operations to figure out how the U.S. military could best mount another attempt. At that time, there were no U.S. helicopter units trained in stealthy, short-notice Special Operations for a quick-reaction mission like the 1st Air Cavalry's air assaults were done in Vietnam.

Night Stalkers

So, what is the legacy of the 1st Air Cavalry division after the Vietnam War? "Air Cavalry" is dramatically portrayed in movies like *Apocalypse Now* and *We Were Soldiers*.

A historian may opine that the 1st Air Cav was the forerunner of present ubiquitous helicopter activity—military operations, search and rescue, hospital medivac, police surveillance, construction with heavy helicopters, forest fire suppression, traffic control, etc. Helicopter operations of raids and air assaults epitomized the Vietnam War and were precursors to similar missions of the 160th SOAR—the "Night Stalkers."

Politics and new missions changed the 1st Air Cavalry; the 160th SOAR, which may be considered to be "air cavalry light," now conducts "airmobile operations." Soldiers, weapons, units, and missions change—it has always been that way; but the legacy of the 1st Air Cavalry continues with variations on the theme.

Since the country's beginning, the U.S. Army continuously evolved and eventually enhanced its missions using "mobility." The 1st Air Cavalry epitomized that progress.

The genesis of the 1st Air Cavalry and its morphing into the Night Stalkers puts Army aviation and airmobile operations into perspective. The Army looked to the 101st Aviation Group, the air arm of the 101st Airborne Division (Air Assault), which had the most experienced helicopter units at the time, and selected elements of the 158th Aviation Battalion, 229th Aviation Battalion, and the 159th Aviation Battalion for new missions. The pilots entered intensive training in night flying.

The provisional unit was first called Task Force 158 since the majority of the pilots were Blackhawk aviators detached from the 158th. The 101st "Screaming Eagle" patches stayed on their uniforms, and the Blackhawks and Chinooks were still used. The OH-6 Cayuses (called LOH for light observation helicopter in Vietnam) had vanished from the division's regular inventory after Vietnam and was in storage and brought back into use.

As the first batch of pilots completed training in the fall of 1980, a second attempt to rescue the hostages in Iran was planned for early 1981. Operation Honey

Badger was called off because the hostages were released on the morning of President Ronald Reagan's inauguration, but the capability gained of ready-reaction airmobile operations was deemed too important for future contingencies to lose.

The new unit was quickly recognized as the Army's best night fighting aviation force and its only Special Operations Aviation force. The pilots and modified aircraft did not return to the 101st; those patches were removed, personnel and equipment were reassigned, and a new tradition was born.

The 160th Special Operations Aviation Regiment (SOAR), otherwise known as Task Force 160 (TF-160) or the "Night Stalkers," are an elite U.S. Army special operations unit that fly helicopters in support of both Special Operations Forces (SOF) and regular forces. Since their beginnings as Task Force 160, following the debacle in Iran, the Night Stalkers have flown missions in Grenada, Panama, the Persian Gulf, Iraq, Kuwait, Afghanistan, and others.

The 160th SOAR was designed and trained to meet new threats. The unit was established on October 16, 1981, and officially designated 160th Aviation Battalion, otherwise known as Task Force 160 (TF-160)—"Night Stalkers."

The Night Stalkers performed enhanced helicopter missions, by emphasizing "night operations" capability with advanced helicopters and equipment. As the 1st Air Cavalry knew, helicopter mobility and firepower were still the key to success.

The following units and equipment are reported as of 2021 but are subject to constant change and improvement. The 160th SOAR fly the following helicopters: MH-47G Chinook, MH-60M Black Hawk, MH-60M DAP (gunship variant), AH-6M/MH-6M Little Bird.

It controls the Q-1C Gray Eagle. The 160th SOAR received its first MQ-1C Gray Eagle company in November 2013, and it now has its own organic unmanned Aircraft Systems platoon. The drone is a copy of the USAF MQ-1 Predator and can carry Hellfire missiles and numerous sensor suites of radars, signal intelligence and high-definition cameras.

160th SOAR missions include insertion/extraction of special operations forces (SOF), attack missions, and reconnaissance. The 160th Special Operations Aviation Regiment mission tactics copied, improved, and were part of the legacy of the 1st Air Cavalry Vietnam War operations and experience involving innovative use of helicopter operations in "air cavalry tactics."

The missions of the historic 1st Air Cavalry Division

were to reconnoiter, screen, delay, and conduct raids over wide terrain. From the 1st Air Cavalry Division to 101st Airmobile Division to 101st Air Assault Division to Task Force 158 to Task Force 160 (TF 160—"Night Stalkers") to 160th Special Aviation Regiment—the personnel, the aircraft, the missions evolved and improved.

The new, action Army came rapidly into the computer age and is constantly being improved and upgraded. In 2016, the Special Operations Aviation-Advanced Tactics Training prepared 160th aircrews and staff personnel testing and validating procedures as follows: Special Operations Mission Survivability (SOAMS) teams accessed and analyzed threats, integrated assets, and executed solutions that supported traditional mission-planning cell.

Intelligence soldiers provided the enemy situation—who, what, where, when, and why. Cyber-electromagnetic activities soldiers showed how to defeat electronic warfare threats from offensive tactics, aircraft survivability equipment use, and integration of electronic warfare assets.

Aviators learned how to develop complex air plans and employ denied-area tactics, techniques and procedures, and mitigating tactical risk.

It is a fair argument that the evolution of the 160th Special Operations Aviation Regiment (160th SOAR) "Night Stalkers" stems from the success of the 1st Air Cavalry Division operations in Vietnam. There is little in-depth history of Army aviation during the Vietnam War because much of it was taken for granted, but today, helicopters are everywhere performing numerous, varied missions.

The contributions of development and effectiveness of the 1st Air Cavalry Division (Airmobile) to Army aviation during the Vietnam War cannot be denied as the 1st Air Cav was the model and set the standard for future airmobile units during Vietnam and future helicopter operations like those employed by the 160th SOAR Night Stalkers.

Women, Racists, and Dissidents in the Military

Man has historically fought the wars while women and children have been protected because war is brutal, ugly, and terrifying; but war's purpose is still basically the same—to impose one's will over another or to acquire or maintain economic benefit or to defend against an adversary. War often involves death—kill or be killed—and destruction.

The basic ground-fighting soldier is called an infantryman. *The mission of the Infantry is to close with the enemy by means of fire and maneuver in order to destroy or capture him, or to repel his assault with fire, close combat, and counterattack.*

In the 1960s, no one could have imagined women in the 1st Air Cavalry Division in Vietnam performing infantry combat missions. After Air Cavalry got to landing zones and dismounted the helicopters to fight as infantry, they hiked long distances, carried heavy loads of equipment, slept on the ground, in the mud, on the sand, ate C-rations, shared experiences, bonded, faced death together, put the dead into body bags, "peed" and "pooped" in the boonies, talked about girls and getting "laid" (sex), and mourned the loss of fellow soldiers.

There were no females in air cavalry (infantry) units in Vietnam for legitimate reasons because men and women perform, bond, celebrate, and mourn differently. Army infantry or Marine infantry units require a special bonding and camaraderie that men have experienced since the dawn of time. The capabilities and bonding among soldiers who trust their lives to each other in a hostile combat environment is essential.

The Vietnam War educated the U.S. about Viet Cong women and Vietnamese children planting explosives, but these actions were done for survival—not as a "jobs program." VC women killed U.S. troops. A women can kill just like a man if her survival depends on it.

Some argue that the U.S. military became more of a "jobs program" rather than an institution for national defense—that in the interests of creating jobs for women, it over-compensated to the detriment of U.S. national security. The following is controversial but consider that the military is to fight wars by neutralizing opposing armed forces.

The emphasis on women in the military presents unique issues, and it is folly for anyone to believe that the military should be simply a jobs program requiring equal opportunity for the sexes. It should not. The ultimate role of the military is to defend this country. Both sexes have their strengths and weaknesses, and some women are very athletic and can perform physical tasks better than many men; but those women are the exceptions to the rule. It is questionable that women have the physical capability to serve in combat in most situations.

Ethan Huff wrote an interesting piece in *Military, News, and Opinions* (2021):

"U.S. Army ends gender neutral fitness test because female soldiers keep failing…"

Huff noted that the Army Combat Fitness Test (ACFT) was designed for both male and female soldiers to have the same set of physical fitness standards, reflecting real-life battlefield conditions.

Steve Beynon wrote on Military.com that the Army was considering adding gender-specific standards to its new Army Combat Fitness Test, or ACFT, after early data shows ***half of female soldiers couldn't pass the test*** and could face removal from service once it became official. Per a Pentagon study, women failed the ACFT at a rate of about 65 percent—compared to just 10 percent for men. Let's be realistic—there are missions for certain combat units that require the strength and endurance of men rather than women.

Matthew Cox wrote for Military.com that another change to the Army Combat Fitness Test rollout plan was to have new enlisted soldiers and commissioned officers taking the test as a graduation requirement starting after Oct. 1, 2021. The latest ACFT adjustments came right after the Army's initial message that the age and gender-neutral ACFT would replace the 40-year-old Army Physical Fitness Test, or APFT.

Army officials assessed ACFT standards, made tweaks and changes as needed, to ensure that the fitness test precisely targeted readiness and combat-related skills for new soldiers. Physical capabilities can be crucial in combat situations, and female soldiers should be capable of fulfilling minimal, relevant physical requirements.

Women in combat units can be disruptive on several levels by causing psychological-sociological problems because group dynamics would drastically change. Men act differently around women—men may seek sex, may be overly protective, or have sexual prejudice against women in a man's unit, or try to show off to impress the females. Small unit tactics, living in the "boonies" or occupying fortified positions (foxholes or bunkers) in life-threatening conditions, are not conducive to healthy male-female relationships.

Privacy and hygiene are different for men and women, and feminine hygiene and emotional stability can be serious issues for women in combat in environmentally hostile areas (mountains, desert, jungle, etc.) especially without the usual amenities of civilization.

Non-ground infantry-type fighting is NOT the same as eating, sleeping, patrolling, joking, sharing experiences, or fighting and dying together in the jungle, forest, mountains, or the desert. Some males are "weeded out" from assignments in various operational or combat units. Women can serve in many positions in the military, perhaps better than men in many instances; but to mandate a quota for women to serve in certain combat units to show egalitarianism in the military is sheer folly. *Women should not be in the infantry.*

More intelligent thought should be directed to the roles of men and women serving together in the military.

Operations Desert Storm and Enduring Freedom gave the U.S. military a reprieve from fighting well-trained military forces in large-scale conventional wars; therefore, females were inserted into the combat zones as helicopter and fighter pilots, Military Police, medical, transportation, maintenance, logistical, and clerical personnel.

Let me be clear about women in the military—with the dissolution of the draft and increased pay for military personnel and relatively weak enemies to challenge the U.S.—the time was right to make the U.S. military more ecumenical, and women should have all the opportunities affordable with military service.

Presently, there are more females in U.S. combat and combat support units; but the world is still unsafe with Latin American and Asian dictators, Russian and Chinese ambitions, and other unknown threats to U.S. national security lurking in the dark.

Time and challenges will tell the results of our social engineering. The services must make intelligent decisions regarding training and assignments for women considering many of the factors previously described.

Sexual harassment and discrimination still infect the military. There should not be sexual harassment or discrimination against females in the military, but ***a female's unwarranted allegations, if untrue, can be devastating to an accused's career.*** The argument for women to serve in combat is moot because "women already serve in combat," but women firing rockets from helicopters or serving on a ship at sea in segregated quarters, or dropping bombs, are not exposed to the close-quarter dangers as the ground units previously stated.

Racists, anarchists, dissidents, or domestic terrorists must be barred from military service. It is a stain on the image of the U.S. military that some of its members planned race riots or other anti-government actions (e.g., 2021 attack on Congress) or destruction and looting of businesses.

There is no place for racism in the U.S. military, but there were military-trained rioters in the Spring 2021 Capitol attack. Racism, whether "white" or "nonwhite," detracts from unit cohesion which is crucial to a combat unit. The military must not be a home for dissidents, racists, anarchists, or domestic terrorists from any group—it must be composed of patriots willing to protect their country and its traditional U.S. Constitutional principles.

My Personal Experience in Vietnam

My Introduction to Vietnam

I was born in Tucson, Arizona, in 1943 and lived there all my life except for one year of college in Iowa, another year at Fort Benning, Georgia, and Fort Polk, Louisiana, and another year in the Republic of Vietnam (January 1968 to 1969).

As a boy, our Mom took my younger brother and me to Veterans Day parades to see the floats, horses, bands, and the veterans from WW I, WW II, and Korea who proudly marched in front of the crowds lining the streets. Grandpa marched in the parade because in the early 1900s, he was a sergeant in the 1st Cavalry which was part of General "Black Jack" Pershing's Punitive Expedition chasing Pancho Villa into Mexico. Grandpa was a proud veteran. Other members of my family also served in the military.

My Uncle Bill was 1st Sergeant, Company H, in the 158th Infantry Regiment in WWII, General Douglass MacArthur's point element (the Bushmasters) in the Philippine Islands campaign. Uncle Bob, my father's younger brother, served with the 34th Infantry in the North African campaign. He worked with the Counter Intelligence Corps because he was fluent in Arabic. He had his gold tooth fillings removed (Bedouins did not have gold tooth fillings), wore Arab garb, and entered Bedouin camps to get intelligence on Nazi unit movements. He carried a .45 cal. "Tommy-gun."

My brother, Bob, was a Medical Service Battalion Commander in Operation Desert Storm, had an interesting career, served 30 years on active duty, and retired as Colonel. My father was deaf due to a childhood illness and could not serve, but he was very proud of his two sons who did.

After Vietnam, veterans did not get those accolades from crowds at parades when they came home. The anecdotes were true about returning Vietnam veterans being spit upon, objects being thrown at them, being taunted, yelled at, and abused. That was America at the time as Vietnam veterans suffered the worst insult of all—they were ignored; and later they were forgotten! I do not know how the country can atone for that sin.

My education was in Tucson—elementary school, high school, both undergraduate and law schools at the University of Arizona. I hiked in the desert and mountains and liked to target practice. I loved and still love the Arizona desert. Undergraduate school was at the University of Arizona in the early 1960s—a great time of drinking and chasing coeds. It was the time of sex, drugs, and rock and roll," "hippies" and "hippie chicks," "acid rock," mini-skirts, muscle cars, James Bond, the *Doors*, the *Animals*, the *Rolling Stones*, the *Beatles, Peter, Paul, and Mary*, etc. I drank lots of alcohol and lots of coffee, but I never smoked pot nor did other drugs.

Despite my hedonism, I was a good student majoring in English, with a split minor in Speech and Sociology. I got good grades while being in a fraternity and captain of the University of Arizona wrestling team before going to Vietnam. Wrestling for eight years (high school and college) helped to develop strength, confidence, and leadership, which I would need to lead infantry troops in combat. Minors in speech and sociology taught me group dynamics and persuasion and were also useful in leading a platoon.

My undergraduate college curriculum was primarily the humanities—the history of western civilization, Greeks and Romans, Homer, Ovid, Aristotle, Socrates, Alexander, and Caesar. Other studies included philosophers, ancient heroes, the Middle Ages, Dante, Descartes, Hume, the Renaissance, religion and philosophical thought, military leaders, and American political history. From that I learned about people.

I was a student of life, an over-achiever, a patriot, a Renaissance man (e.g., scholar, athlete, philosopher, soldier) in a hedonistic society. The Vietnam War was escalating, the U.S. had a draft in those days, so I enrolled in the advanced Army ROTC program in college allowing me to serve my country as an officer. I liked ROTC at the U of A, especially the training in patrolling, and was a distinguished Military Graduate in 1965.

I attended a year of law school, a semester of graduate school in business, and went on active duty in 1967.

Be Careful What You Wish For

After the Combat Platoon Leaders Course (CPLC) at Fort Benning, I "pushed troops" as a training officer at Fort Polk, Louisiana for several months, which was a valuable experience and training for me. I still wonder which was a more arduous tour—serving during Tet 1968 in Vietnam or serving at Fort Polk, Leesville, Louisiana with some Southern folks still fighting the Civil War.

My parents saw me off from my flight from Tucson. It was a serious matter as my parents sent their son off to war. My Ma could tell I was apprehensive, and she smiled and said, "Don't worry, you'll be alright and come home." I kissed my mother, shook hands with my father, and boarded the plane for a new adventure.

I flew from Tucson to Travis Air Force Base in the San Francisco Bay area via commercial flight, and from Travis AFB I flew to the Republic of Vietnam on a military aircraft—a C-130. I was not going to be a "draft-dodger." I wanted to lead men in combat. I exited the plane in Vietnam on January 6, 1968, and it was a hot, humid, stifling heat unlike the dry heat I grew up with in Arizona.

We got into a bus with heavy screening on the windows so hand grenades could not be thrown into the vehicle. The driver drove rapidly through the streets and we all were concerned about ambushes or terrorist attacks. I was educated, but I think that was when it dawned on me that I was truly in a war zone. We got to the in-processing location where we stayed several days sleeping on cots and waiting for our assignments and destinations.

I was assigned as 2nd platoon leader, D Company, 2nd Battalion, 7th Cavalry, 1st Cavalry Division (Airmobile). We were airmobile infantry—an entire division of helicopters. Our mission was to kill or capture the enemy by means of fire and maneuver. A helicopter took me to the top of a hill to link up with my platoon to begin a "year of living dangerously."

In 1968, the civil rights movement was in full swing, and racism existed in the U.S. and the Army, and those racial tensions went to Vietnam, too. About a quarter to a third of my platoon was a minority at various times (no women) as troops rotated in and out.

I did not tolerate any racial discrimination or favoritism. Being of Lebanese descent, I was sensitive to ethnic diversity. As an athlete in high school and college, competing with and against various minorities, I learned to respect people for their abilities and positive contributions. I had a Black platoon sergeant; and my best "point man" and my battalion commander, LTC Robinson, were Black. Robinson later became a four-star general. This sounds like, "Some of my best friends were Black," but it was what it was.

Young men who were drafted may not have had a college education, or may have come from farms or the inner city, or were Black, Brown, poor-White, "Hill Billy," Puerto Rican; but they were the best soldiers the U.S. ever had. It is a national disgrace that they were treated and defamed as they were when they came home.

The Tet offensive occurred January 30 and 31, 1968, during the Chinese Lunar New Year. It was a major Viet Cong (VC) and North Vietnamese Army (NVA) uprising in South Vietnam. The effect of televised carnage of war in near real-time was horrendous, and it caused negative American public opinion as evidenced by the increase in antiwar protests.

The Vietnam War was brutal, especially for the

ground combatants. Vietnam veterans saw far more action than did WW II veterans; and they won all the battles and came home to a radical, hostile, ungrateful antimilitary populace. South Vietnam surrendered to Communist forces two years after U.S. forces left and a peace treaty was signed.

The Vietnam War was actually two wars at the same time—the war in-country in the jungles, hills, mountains, waterways, and in the air. It was also the war throughout the USA on television, radio, movies, news reports, history classes, college campuses, and on the streets. The U.S. combatants had to fight two wars.

The Tet Offensive

Khe Sanh and the Beginning of Tet

In early 1968, there were indications that something was brewing around Khe Sanh. The location in northwest South Vietnam made Khe Sanh a base for allied operations against Communist infiltration of men and supplies into the south although it was encircled by enemy troops. On January 21, 1968, the siege of 6,000 Marines who were surrounded by 20,000 North Vietnamese troops began at Khe Sanh Combat Base.

Khe Sanh was strategically and politically important to the U.S. because it was located about fifteen miles south of the Demilitarized Zone and barely seven miles from the eastern frontier of Laos. To the south, Khe Sanh overlooked Highway 9, the only east-west road in the Northern Province to join Laos and the coastal regions.

General Westmoreland and the Marines who manned Khe Sanh carried out a campaign to block North Vietnamese infiltration into South Vietnam by way of the Demilitarized Zone that divided the two Vietnams. They also built up a base area to serve as a jumping-off point for an U.S. advance (if authorized) into the panhandle region of Laos to cut off the Ho Chi Minh Trail.

If the U.S. abandoned Khe Sanh, entire North Vietnamese divisions could pour down Route 9 (the major east-west highway below the DMZ) and four other natural approaches through the valleys and overrun a chain of Marine positions.

If the Rockpile, Con Thien, Dong Ha, and Phu Bai to the east were overrun, the NVA could be in a good position to seize control of South Vietnam's two northernmost provinces, Quang Tri and Thua Thien, with severe political and psychological results. A key feature of the base was a 3,900-foot aluminum mat runway.

President Johnson and his advisors were terrified for weeks that the siege of Khe Sanh would be the prelude to a full-scale assault on the Marine Combat Base at Khe Sanh, comparable to General Giap's 1954 Viet Minh victory over the French at a similar base at Dien Bien Phu.

On January 30 and 31, 1968, the Tet Offensive began and was a coordinated series of NVA attacks on more than 100 cities and towns in South Vietnam. The

Communists intended to cause rebellion by the South Vietnamese and encourage the U.S. to scale back its involvement in the Vietnam War. The Viet Cong simultaneously attacked numerous, mostly populated areas with heavy U.S. troop presence. They breached walls of the U.S. Embassy in Saigon for a short time; but U.S. and ARVN forces held off the attacks.

Prejudicial news coverage of the massive offensive shocked the American public and diminished support for the war. Communist strikes on major cities like Hue and Saigon had a strong psychological impact showing that VC troops were not as weak as the Johnson Administration claimed. The U.S. and ARVN units actually won the Tet battles.

The North Vietnamese Army (NVA) captured portions of Hue Citadel, with the intent to "liberate" the entire city as part of a countrywide popular uprising to sweep the VC into power. Hue residents and other South Vietnamese shunned the Communists who seized the city and committed atrocities on the people. Because of this, politicians, policemen, military, farmers, old women, young girls, and children were executed and buried in mass graves.

The U.S. media and antiwar protesters never acknowledged the murder of over 5800 civilians; their hands were tied behind their backs; chained together; and killed by the Communists; but they grudgingly acknowledged that the U.S. and ARVN were the victors during Tet. The media grossly misrepresented Tet as there was sparse reporting about Communist atrocities.

Beginning January 22, 1968, allied airmen dropped 80,000 tons of ordnance around Khe Sanh, more than the nonnuclear tonnage dropped on Japan throughout World War II, but the bombing had limited effectiveness. Air power bombing is essential but not always the final solution. Relentless bombing had not stopped enemy movement around Khe Sanh; and the Marines at Khe Sanh were still clearly under siege.

On February 6 and 7, the North Vietnamese used amphibious light tanks to attack Lang Vei and overran the Special Forces camp located just 7 kilometers (4.3 miles) from Khe Sanh. At the base, two Marine companies could not deploy to rescue Lang Vei because the NVA controlled Route Nine, and the NVA were deadly.

On February 8, NVA gunners fired hundreds of mortar rounds into a Marine position on a nearby hill followed by an assault that resulted in 21 men killed, 26 wounded and four Marines missing in action. During the previous week, the enemy had managed to fire

1,500 rocket, artillery and mortar rounds at the Khe Sanh base.

On February 21, during the rainy season, I flew from Camp Evans to near an old French compound (maybe a convent or monastery) between Hue and the DMZ. Our company was located at an old French compound providing security for 8-inch guns (8-inch diameter shells) and 175-mm artillery batteries that gave fire support to the Marines and some 1st Cav units fighting at Hue.

Hue was the ancient Imperial Capital of Vietnam—a beautiful, walled imperial city with a great history. I think we were only around 25 "clicks" (kilometers) from Hue, which had suffered intense fighting. We were right near Highway 1 on the main supply line to Hue and had set up a defensive perimeter with the artillery.

The Tet Offensive was conducted by the Communists in the hopes of achieving a decisive victory that would end the grinding conflict that frustrated military leaders on both sides. They thought that a successful attack on major cities might force the United States to negotiate or perhaps even to withdraw.

At the very least, the North Vietnamese hoped it would serve to stop the ongoing escalation of guerilla attacks and bombing in the North. Hanoi selected the

Tet holiday to strike because it was traditionally a time of truce, and because Vietnamese traveling to spend the festival with their relatives provided cover for the movement of South North Vietnamese Army (NVA) and the NLF (National Liberation Forces) or Viet Cong.

The ensuing 26-day effort by the U.S. Marines, U.S. Army, and South Viet Nam Army (ARVN) to recapture the Hue Citadel produced a stunning military defeat for the invaders, but the U.S. media grossly misrepresented this fact. The "strategic victory" during Tet ultimately went to the Communists because the media led by Walter Cronkite misinformed the American public about the U.S. success in the fighting in Tet and Hue.

Although the U.S. military and the Army of the Republic of Vietnam (ARVN) won all the major battles, there was little reporting about those successes and the Communist atrocities. The scenes of bloody fighting in Hue, Saigon, and other cities in Vietnam during Tet really shocked the American people who experienced war for the first time on their television sets, and the pressure to withdraw from the war became overwhelming. America needed a "win" that the media would report—maybe something like the cavalry riding to the rescue of a besieged fort as portrayed in an old Western movie.

Vietnam Was A Just War

On February 25, the day after the ARVN troops pulled down the Viet Cong flag flying over the Citadel at Hue, 1st Cavalry D Company, HQ, 1st, 2nd, and 3rd Platoon, swept the nearby area around the old French compound about 7 to 10 miles northwest of Hue. We moved in a column-formation through the villages looking for VC and NVA troops. We were on point and were fired at several times that day. The sniper shots came close because we could hear the twang as they went by or the crack of the bullets as they broke the sound barrier.

The monsoon-season was miserable as we hiked in mud and high humidity. We conducted "sweeps" through jungle, on the sand along the coast, crossed streams and rice paddies, and searched villages—the houses, hooches, or huts. We looked for VC, NVA, weapons, or rice caches, which were their food supply. In highly vegetated areas, my platoon moved along in a column, or single file, or a modified column, which was an oval-looking formation, if the terrain allowed.

When we crossed open areas, rice paddies, or along the sand, or if we were in an assault phase, I put the platoon in an "online" formation—a straight lateral line with weapons forward for maximum firepower. Our weapons were always "at the ready." Many of us took a hand grenade ring from the pin, attached it to the front rifle sight of our M-16s, and tied a nylon cord or shoelace to that ring and to the stock's rear.

We slung the improvised sling (shoe-lace) over our shoulders and had our shooting hand on the pistol grip of the rifle and our thumb on the selector switch of the rifle ready to flick it from "safety" to "semi" to "auto." But my main job was to lead and direct my platoon, not to fire my M-16. I loved the M-16 and qualified "expert" with it.

February 27, 1968—My Epiphany

By the end of February, I was in-country for around seven weeks and had learned how to lead my Air Cavalry platoon and how to keep us all alive. We had been sniped at and mortared, but no significant contact, yet. Occasionally, we heard the U.S. artillery fire missions in support of units near Hue.

The Marines and a few units of the 1st Cav were in heavy combat at Hue. The Marines did a good job in liberating the ancient capitol, but a few Marines, whom Walter Cronkite interviewed, expressed uniformed, ignorant political views maligning the merits of U.S. involvement in Vietnam and damning the action at Hue.

Walter Cronkite originally had a positive report about U.S. action there, but on February 27, *he changed his original report about how well U.S. troops did* at Hue to a critical, pessimistic view that the U.S. should call it a draw and go home.

Joe Abodeely

Hue Citadel

Communist sympathizers and media accepted and publicized that report which was a major factor in demoralizing the U.S. public and causing support for U.S. action in Vietnam to plummet.

On February 27, my company commander called me over to his command post and said, "Skeeter" (as he called me and as we looked at a map), "I want you to take your platoon and go north along the river." We were hoping to make contact with the enemy. Patrolling was serious business because we left the security of a base camp.

I got my platoon ready—we checked our weapons, ammo, Claymore mines, smoke and fragmentation grenades, ponchos and poncho liners, gear, radios, SOI (signal operating instructions), and C-rations. We walked out of the base camp perimeter and proceeded on our mission. What we carried depended on the mission.

It had been raining for days, but the sun was out this day. My platoon moved along in relatively open areas in 3 modified squad columns for ease of movement, control, and security. I formed the platoon into three squads—each squad had a PRC-25 radio, and I had two RTOs (radio/telephone operators) with PRC-25s with me for constant communication.

When we got into the jungle, we went into single file with a few troops posted as flank security. As we moved along, my RTOs and I stayed behind the lead squad—about a third of the way back in the second squad in order of movement—for the best command and control and reaction capability.

We came to a deserted village which was eerie because nobody was around. No "mamasons," no "babysons." There was only an old man who had his nose cut off sitting on the trail as we approached. His face had a triangle scar where his nose should be (like the triangle cut in a Halloween pumpkin). He told us that there were no VC (Viet Cong) in the area. Sergeant Duk (pronounced Duke), my ARVN interpreter, did the questioning; and neither Duk nor I believed this guy. He was extremely nervous. We left him and moved through the empty village. It was ominous that no one else was around.

As we moved along on our patrol, we were still in a platoon column formation. We all stopped to eat lunch (our C-rations); hearing "small-arms" fire up in front of the lead squad, I went forward to the point squad to see what was happening. He told me that he saw what appeared to be an ARVN who fired at him. He thought the "shooter" wasn't a "friendly."

The ARVNs were the soldiers of the Republic of South Viet Nam—the people we were there to protect from the NVA and Viet Cong. My point man said he shot at the "ARVN" and thought he hit him.

We moved ahead to a small ditch and saw some fresh blood on the ground, which indicated that the "ARVN" had been hit. At about the same time, a small "bubble" chopper flew overhead nearby, and we heard automatic weapons fire, apparently directed at the chopper. I did not want to pursue the "ARVN," who I thought fired at the chopper to lead us away from following the river as we headed north.

We continued along the river until we got to a road, which went over a small wooden bridge over a small stream. It was a nice pastoral image. There were trees and other thick foliage around the bridge and a small running stream. The platoon carefully and quickly crossed the bridge and assembled around an abandoned stone house surrounded by trees and other vegetation.

There was an open rice paddy-clearing with a tree line and stone buildings approximately a couple hundred meters away on the side of the house opposite our location.

The point man came back to my location and said,

"2-6, I just saw about twelve or thirteen NVA moving along in a trench" off to our left front. The call sign, "2-6," was my nickname. The "2" meant "second platoon," and the "6" meant "leader."

He assured me they were NVA because of their khaki uniforms and pith helmets and that they were running apparently intending to ambush us on our left flank. I rushed to get everyone assembled in a good defensive position around the house because we weren't dug in and were extremely vulnerable.

Suddenly, all hell broke loose! RPG (rocket-propelled grenade) rounds started coming in, exploding on the other side of the stone house. Automatic weapons fire seemed to come continuously from our left front, front, and right front. Bullets were popping by us no matter where we moved. The point man and his backup point man were returning fire, but they were out in the open ahead of the rest of us.

I saw the point man lying in a prone position pumping out a lot of rounds from his M-16, and I saw a bullet hit his steel pot (helmet) throwing sparks as it glanced off.

His backup point man stood up behind him and fired several rounds. Suddenly, the backup point man got hit in the arm and in the torso and went down.

Some of us were able to get into one of the NVA trenches near our position as the bullets were coming from everywhere. We expended a lot of ammo returning fire.

A firefight is pandemonium. The dut-dut-dut-dut-dut-dut of automatic weapons fire; the popping and whizzing of incoming small-arms fire, the explosions of incoming rocket propelled grenades, and the firing of our 90-mm recoilless rifle were the dramatic, terrifying sounds of war. A blond kid we called "Smitty" was firing his M-60 machine gun from behind an old leafless tree.

He was standing up making the machine gun spew forth its "rain of bullets" as fast as the metal links of the ammunition belt would allow the linked bullets to pass without jamming the gun. He was not behind sufficient cover and took a round clean through his arm. We got him to our location in the trench, gave him morphine, and he slept throughout the rest of the firefight which was intense as we were surrounded.

The wounded backup point man was lying on the ground behind the point man who was still returning fire. The only way to retrieve him was to leave the safety of the trench and get him. As scared as we were, my platoon sergeant, medic, and I crawled out of the trench under heavy enemy fire (bullets "popping" everywhere), and we dragged the wounded soldier back to the trench.

He was gurgling because as he was shot in the arm, he spun around and was shot in the lung. I heard later that he got transported to Tokyo and lived. I now had five men wounded—three were hit with the first in-coming RPG rounds.

The artillery forward observer who came along with us was trying desperately to get some artillery support for us. He kept calling on his radio for artillery, but all the guns were trained on Hue because there had been a lot of action going on around there, so we couldn't get artillery. I had a firestorm to contend with. We were completely surrounded by a much larger and entrenched force; I had wounded men; and we could not get artillery support. Things were not good.

At one point we tried to see if we could get back across the bridge. I originally asked a young sergeant to take a few men to see if they could cross the bridge; he said, "Sir, we'll get killed if we go out there." I was the platoon leader; so, as scared as I was, I knew I was going to have to lead a few men to check out a withdrawal route.

I took my RTO and a few other men, and we slowly eased out of the NVA trench and low-crawled to a furrowed field. Bullets were still flying and "snapping" and "popping" everywhere as we hugged the earth for dear life. As our mini patrol eased back toward the little wooden bridge, two snipers in trees at the bridge started firing at us and pinned us down, so we couldn't move.

The RTO was able to contact an ARA (aerial rocket artillery helicopter gunship)—a Huey armed with rocket pods and two M-60 door-gunners. We were the 1st Air Cav, so we had the lift ships to haul troops and supplies; and we had the gunships—the ARAs—on call for fire support. While the snipers kept us pinned down, we lay flat in the furrows of the field; and I could hear the snap of the bullets breaking the sound barrier as they passed nearby.

We hugged those furrows for dear life as we directed the ARA to fire on the trees with the snipers. When the helicopter made a couple of passes firing rockets, the screaming hiss of the rockets, which seemed to go right over our heads, convinced me we would be hit by "friendly fire." I just knew they would hit us—but they didn't. The gunship did a good job of hitting where we told him, but the snipers were still there. We crawled back to the trench after the unsuccessful attempt to get back across the bridge.

The firefight continued, but at one point, we called in a couple medivac choppers for our wounded. My platoon sergeant and I used machetes to try to clear a LZ (landing zone) prior to their arrival so they could land. We left our cover, stood up, and hacked at saplings and brush; and we made a suitable LZ to pick up our wounded.

For some mysterious reason, the NVA firing lightened up as we were clearing the area and were clearly exposed to potential enemy fire. As the medivac helicopters descended and then landed, the NVA quit firing. My platoon sergeant and I helped the crewmen load the five wounded troopers on the choppers.

Maybe the NVA were maneuvering for better positions, or maybe they were gathering their wounded or maybe they recognized the big Red Cross on the front of the medivac ships and honored the Geneva Conventions. After the medivac choppers were in the air, out of the fighting, and on their way back to save lives, the firing started up again—to this day, I don't know why the NVA stopped shooting when they did.

While all of these events were occurring, we notified Heavy Bones 6 (my CO), who was bringing the first, third, and mortar platoons up to give us some support. It seemed to take forever for them to get to our location, but the jungle was thick, and they did not know exactly where we were. Finding something in the thick jungle is like finding a needle in a haystack. So very trite, but so very true.

Prior to the rest of the company's arrival, we were able to get some "4-Deuce" fire support. I never really appreciated the effectiveness of the 4.2-inch mortar until that day when those 4.2-inch mortar rounds were called in, and the shells came crashing down in the open rice paddy and tree line in front of us.

The explosions were tremendous—trees were flying, smoke was rising—the thump-thump, thump-thump was rhythmic. A 4.2-inch round is like a 105-mm howitzer round, but it is 106.6-mm (even bigger). So, we finally got our artillery, after all—from a huge mortar.

As the CO (Heavy Bones 6) got closer to our location, he tried to pinpoint where we were. We generally guided him to our location over the radio, but it was difficult for the rest of the company to know where we were because we had traveled through some thick jungle; now, we were taking cover in NVA trenches.

To make matters even worse, first platoon was reconning by fire as they were approaching us from our right rear. "Reconning by fire" was shooting randomly into the jungle as they advanced in our direction to secure their path of approach.

Now, we had to worry about getting hit by our own guys. We stayed low, and eventually Delta Company (my company) got to the tree line to the right of the NVA as we observed them. My platoon laid down a base of fire as the rest of the company maneuvered. We let loose with our M-16s, M-60s, and M-79 grenade launchers.

After the rest of the company swept through the enemy positions, we all regrouped south of the wooden bridge. Delta had run into what was estimated to be an NVA company or regimental headquarters based on the weapons, communications, and equipment found. It was right on the direct supply line to Hue. Some of the guys told me that there was commo wire all over the place, indicating a major headquarters. The Cav troopers killed an NVA officer, and one of them took his 9-mm pistol as a souvenir.

We had to get a good distance away from the target area to call in an air strike to level the whole area. I think we had moved about a click (1,000 meters) when a jet roared in and dropped its thunderous payload. We were in a prone position on the ground when the extremely loud explosion occurred, and the ground shook.

After the bomb blast, I heard this whirling-buzzing sound heading my way. Then a "plop." About a 6-inch by 5-inch chunk of metal fragment from the bomb landed about two feet from my leg and was still smoldering in the dirt.

My CO and the mortar platoon leader said I did a really good job that day. I recommended a Silver Star for my point man, and he got it . Other decorations were also awarded—none to me. I heard I was put in for a Silver Star, but the executive officer in the rear area nixed it. He was an OCS (officer candidate school graduate) without a college degree, and I think he resented me because of my education.

The greatest award I got in Vietnam was the satisfaction that I lead my men the way an infantry officer is supposed to lead, but more importantly, I kept them all alive. The day had been terrifying, exhilarating, challenging, ultra-stressful, and emotionally draining. I learned a lot about infantry tactics, the meaning of life, and myself from that experience. It was my epiphany.

After the mortar platoon leader and another soldier came over to compliment me, I went over behind a big tree so nobody could see me and cried. I just let out everything I was holding in.

I had five guys wounded; none killed. It was that

day that I made up my mind I would not lose any of my men if I could help it. By the end of my tour, I had kept my promise.

Perhaps one my life's greatest achievements was serving in the 1st Air Cavalry Division, which had the most casualties in Vietnam during Tet 1968 (the bloodiest year of the war), and not losing a man. They all lived when I was in command. Life is precious.

While my whole company, platoon, and I had experienced what I just described on February 27, 1968, Walter Cronkite gave the most misleading and devastating media broadcast about the war:

> *"We Are Mired in Stalemate...*[1]
>
> *Who won and who lost in the great Tet Offensive against the cities? I'm not sure. The Vietcong did not win by a knockout, but neither did we. The referees of history may make it a draw... Khe Sanh could well fall, with a terrible loss in American lives, prestige, and morale, and this is a tragedy of our stubbornness there; but the bastion no longer is a key to the rest of the northern regions, and it is doubtful that the American forces can be defeated across the breadth of the DMZ with any substantial loss of ground. Another standoff...*

1. Excerpts from Walter Cronkite. See Credits.

Vietnam Was A Just War

To say that we are mired in stalemate seems the only realistic, yet unsatisfactory, conclusion... But it is increasingly clear to this reporter that the only rational way out then will be to negotiate, not as victors, but as an honorable people who lived up to their pledge to defend democracy..."

On March 25, a Marine patrol was halted by enemy machine-gun and mortar fire after traveling only 100 to 200 yards past Khe Sanh's barbed-wire perimeter. The Marine two-squad patrol, which was instructed not to venture farther than 1,000 meters from the Khe Sanh perimeter, vanished. Two weeks later, casualties of the so-called "ghost patrol" were established as nine dead, 25 wounded, and 19 missing.

On March 30, a Marine company-size patrol had the mission to recover the bodies of the ghost patrol. This second patrol incurred three dead, 71 wounded, and three missing before being ordered to pull back. Only two bodies from the ghost patrol were recovered at that time. Lieutenant Jaques was killed leading a patrol.

In late March, my battalion, 2/7 Cavalry, got the word we were going to Khe Sanh. My parents sent me newspaper clippings about the Marines at Khe Sanh.

The press portrayed a dire situation, and I thought that if there were a place on earth like being in HELL—it was Khe Sanh. I was concerned about this mission.

Diary and Recollections About Khe Sanh

Operation Pegasus (Relief of Khe Sanh siege)

Planning for the overland relief of Khe Sanh had begun as early as January 25, 1968 when Westmoreland ordered General John J. Tolson, commander, First Cavalry Division, to prepare a contingency plan. Route 9, the only practical overland route from the east, was impassable due to its poor state of repair and the presence of NVA troops.

The following is based on my recollections, a diary, and letters I sent home.

On **April 1, 1968**, I was the oldest of the company's platoon leaders since I finished college, got commissioned as 2nd Lieutenant through ROTC, and then entered active duty. I was 2nd platoon leader in the 2/7 Cav (my battalion, part of the 3rd Brigade of the 1st Cavalry Division) which went by chopper to LZ Calu (Stud)—the main staging area for Operation Pegasus.

Operation Pegasus: Landing Zone Cà Lu (Stud).

ARC Light near Khe Sanh, 1968.

Hundreds of Air Cavalry troops gathered at this location. We assembled our troops to be helicopter-lifted to LZ Calu and then to LZ Thor.

I saw bomb strikes in the distance at night—"Arc Lights," B-52 carpet bombing of NVA troops and materiel, as the sky lit up and the ground shook. It was exciting and scary.

On **April 2**, we air assaulted to a mountain top which was grassy and jungle; the mountain was surrounded by a river on three sides. The weather was nice. I was comfortable sleeping in my poncho liner that night. When we arrived, I jumped from the chopper and hurt my arm—but took it in stride. We, D Company, got a log (logistic) ship (helicopter) with food and water.

At 1700 hrs in the afternoon, D Company led the air assault as we flew to a location closer to Khe Sanh. When we were in the air, prior to dismounting the helicopters, I saw a downed jet in a ravine below and thought that if the NVA could shoot down jets, they certainly could shoot down helicopters. I sat right behind the pilots viewing forward; as we descended, I saw the ground getting closer and closer and closer.

The choppers approached a bombed-out clearing, which would be our landing zone (LZ), pock-marked with craters from aerial bombardment by U.S. airpower.

We dismounted (we used to say "un-assed) the helicopters and took cover in gigantic bomb craters left by massive B-52 bombing. My platoon was on point (lead platoon) for the ground movement, so I assembled them into a modified platoon column formation and we moved out to recon the area.

We did not carry our "butt packs," but we had web gear, C-rations, fragmentation and smoke grenades, Claymore mines, ammunition, M-16s, M-60 machineguns, LAWs (light antitank weapons), PRC-25s (radios), and a 90-mm recoilless rifle. My M-79 grenadiers previously traded in their M-79 grenade launchers for 12-gauge pump shotguns with buckshot or flechette shotgun shells because the jungle was very thick where we were going. The M-79 rounds had to travel a certain distance before they armed, and thick jungle prevented this. The shotguns were great for close-range combat.

Many of us took a hand grenade ring from the pin in the grenade handle and attached it to the front rifle sight of our M-16s. Then we tied a nylon cord or shoelace from the ring to the rear of the rifle stock to put the strap over our shoulders.

We had our thumb on the selector switch for firing mode. In those days, we did not have a "governor" that only allowed four-round bursts as our troops had later. If a troop held his finger on the trigger in full-automatic mode, the weapon could expend a twenty-round magazine in seconds. My job was to lead and direct my platoon, not to fire my M-16, but I did both. Some of us wore flak vests, but we avoided doing so whenever we could. The vests wouldn't stop bullets, but they gave limited protection against small shrapnel and made good pillows for sleeping on the ground.

Most importantly, we carried an extra pair of dry socks. We may have been "air cavalry," but we were still basically infantry, ground troops.

We air assaulted to the top of a mountain.

The terrain was thick, mountainous, jungle, and grassy. We looked for VC, NVA, or weapons. In deep vegetation, we moved in column or file formations, or a modified column, which was an oval-looking formation, if the terrain allowed.

I had a certain sense of being "in the now"—overly alert and attuned to my surroundings—the sights, sounds, and even the smells during operations.

It may sound corny, but I think I was frequently clairvoyant. Infantry-combat veterans will understand what I am saying!

My point man was a guy we called "Hippy." He was

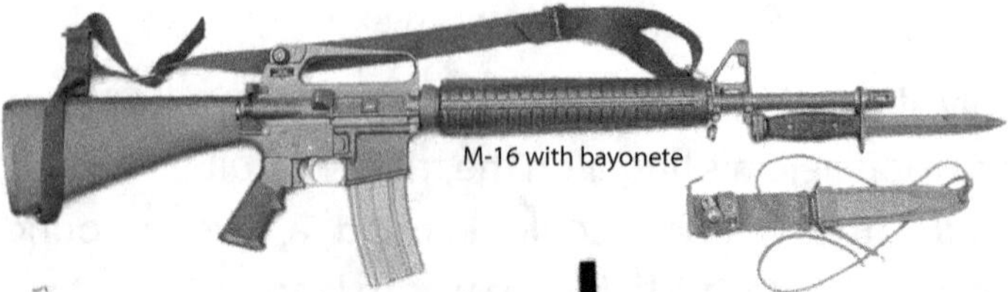

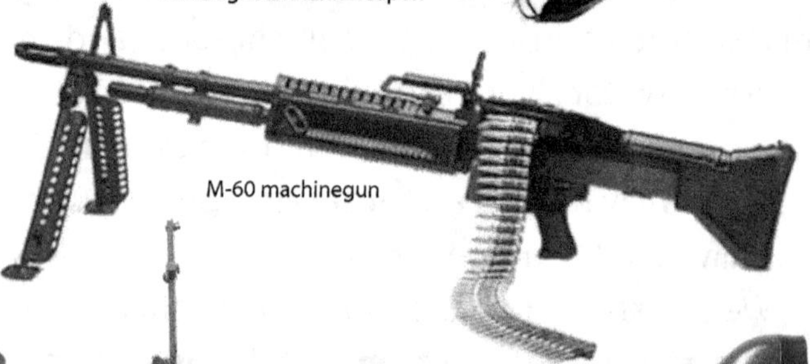

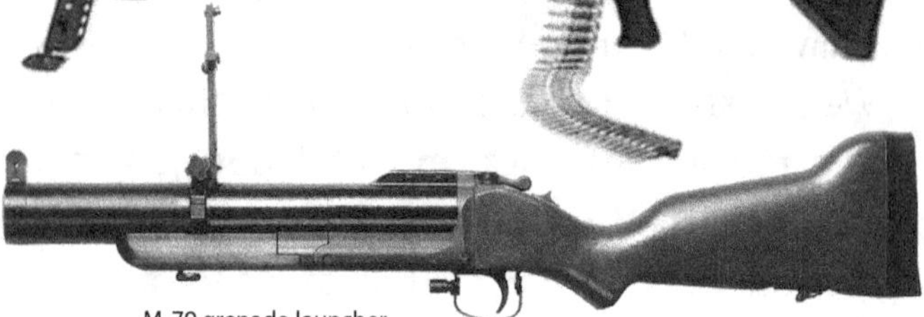

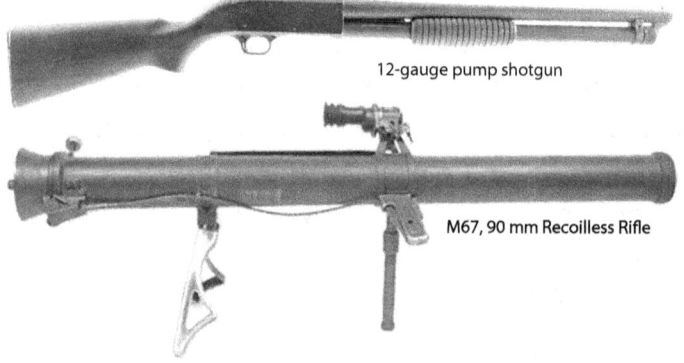

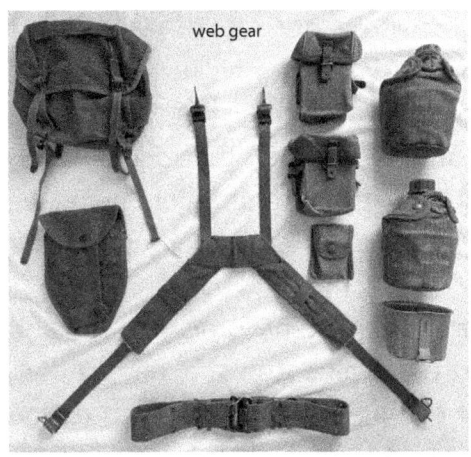

web gear

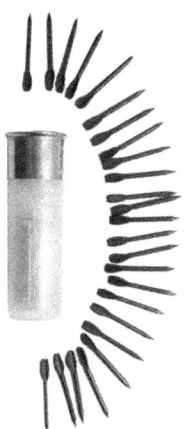

12-ga. flechette round

smoke & frag

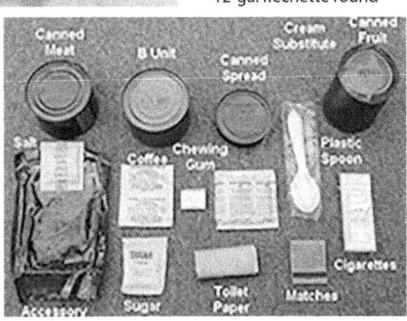

C-rations

claymore mine

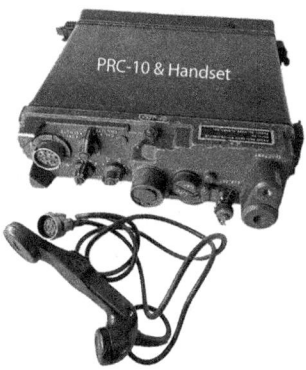

PRC-10 & Handset

lanky and had a peace symbol on his helmet, but he was an excellent point man—the first guy in order of movement as we moved through the jungle. When he gave the signal to halt in a column formation, we all crouched or got down and looked around in 360 degrees.

He hand-signaled, and I went to his location and saw that he found a machine gun site, an NVA helmet, and a bag of raw opium. The NVA used opium for medicinal purposes and perhaps to prepare themselves for sapper (suicide) attacks. I told Hippy to take the bag back to turn it in. I don't know if he did. We continued the patrol and set up camp later that day.

When we crossed open areas or rice paddies or trudged along the sands, or if we were in an assault phase, my platoon was "on line"—a straight lateral line with weapons aimed forward for maximum firepower.

On **April 3**, our whole company (three rifle platoons and the mortar platoon) moved through dense jungle in a company column formation like a large snake winding through the jungle. The foliage was very thick greatly limiting our visibility. Third platoon was "on point" for this movement, and as the company moved through the jungle, we were strung out over a long distance.

We heard shooting and explosions when third platoon made contact (got into a firefight) with the NVA as the semi-and fully-automatic weapons fire and explosions announced the combat up ahead through the jungle. The vegetation was thick, but thankfully, the rich, soft upturned dirt from the bomb explosions made gigantic craters and great pre-dug foxholes.

The NVA had a special knack of dragging away their casualties immediately so that, although you knew you hit someone, when you checked for the bodies, they were gone. It was ominous. It was as though the NVA were ghosts.

When the automatic weapons firing occurred, a popular NCO in 3rd platoon went to retrieve an enemy RPD (light machine gun) for a souvenir and was killed. The S-3 (operations officer) brought him back over his shoulder and set him down close to me.

As the S-3 set the dead soldier down nearby on the ground, the body started regurgitating—the involuntary action after death. I never saw that before, and I will never forget it. Jungle combat was not glamorous; if you weren't scared, you were not paying attention. Combat is terrifying, but the remedy is to concentrate on your mission to forget that you could be killed at any time.

People did not shoot at us; bushes shot at us. I often had bouts with internal terror, but I could not show fear, so I masked it as I lead about 40 men, trying to keep them alive while at the same time performing the missions we were given. I never knew if or when I would become (what we sarcastically called in macabre humor) "maggot meat."

The NVA were great fighters who fought the Japanese, later the French, and then the Americans, but we won all the major combat actions, and we were able to control the area we chose to control. Comparing our time in combat, the quality of the enemy, and our success in combat, we were the best combatants our country ever had.

But it seemed that back home in the U.S, nobody cared about us fighting and dying for our country. On our PRC-25 field radios, we could get *Radio Saigon* and hear about the antiwar protests back in the ungrateful nation that sent us to war.

In the late afternoon, we moved to Hill-242 near Route 9 and set up a company-size perimeter. We started clearing a Landing Zone (LZ) because we wanted to get resupplies from helicopters. We were in a combination of jungle and forest, so we had to clear trees. We wrapped "det cord" (detonation cord, which burns at thousands of feet per second) around smaller trees and blew them down, but there were too many bigger trees; and we could not clear an LZ.

Eventually, the NVA surrounded us in the jungle but, apparently, did not have the force or will to attack us directly. One of the other units took a mule (small flatbed utility vehicle) and tried to bring us supplies along the road. They were ambushed—some were KIA—so we didn't get food or water except for rainwater which we gathered on ponchos tied to trees to catch it.

Using our entrenching tools (folding shovels) and machetes, we created a perimeter defense by digging fox-holes with overhead cover fortifications with tree limbs and logs. As we worked on the defensive positions, we got mortared; about 10 or 11 of my men got minor wounds from mortar shrapnel.

We called for a Medivac helicopter. The wounded were extracted from our position by a jungle penetrator (like a heavy plumb bob to sit on) dropped through the canopy since the jungle was too thick for the Medivac to land. All of the troops were treated and quickly returned to duty.

On one occasion, my platoon sergeant and I were checking our perimeter in the thick jungle overgrowth. I always personally checked all of our perimeter defenses to ensure we did it right whether we were in the jungle, on the sands, in the forests, or on mountains.

As the sergeant and I looked out of our perimeter into the dense jungle, we heard that distinctive "clank" of the bolt of an AK-47 being pulled back. I yelled, "Get down," and we pancaked to the ground as the automatic weapon's fire started chopping the leaves above, which fell on us. The sergeant had a look of terror on his face, and I let out a stupid laugh probably to mask my horror.

Fortunately, when that AK opened-up, one of my young Black troopers started pumping his M-60 fire into the direction of the enemy fire. He must have expended most of a belt of ammo as that M-60 just kept spewing automatic weapon's fire and never jammed once. Prior to heading to Khe Sanh, I went to supply to see to it that my platoon got two new M-60 machine guns; and I was really glad that this trooper took great care of his new M-60 because they could jam when you most needed them. He probably saved my life.

After that incident, we continued working and finished our fortifications. Our perimeter was company size. Visualize a circle of fighting positions for about 150 soldiers, four men per position. We made a perimeter of fighting positions about 10 meters apart as best the terrain would allow in thick jungle.

That night, we heard what sounded like unexploded artillery impacts near the position of my two RTOs (radio men) and me. I heard the company commander say softly over the radio (like a whisper) that it appeared that NVA artillery rounds landed in our perimeter but did not explode. He said that they could be "duds" or chemical agents. I stayed awake all night thinking I'd die from a nerve agent. Obviously, I didn't.

On **April 4**, we moved back to a position where the 105-mm howitzers had been brought in by Chinook helicopters to get supplies. I learned to appreciate the value of our artillery support in Vietnam. At Fort Benning and at Fort Polk, I saw artillery fire in training exercises, but now this was real. I eventually became adept at calling in artillery fire.

An artillery Lieutenant taught me how to call-in artillery fire, and I eventually became incredibly good at it. Artillery could form a wall of steel around my platoon when we were out on patrol in the middle of nowhere. They say, "necessity is the mother of invention;" perhaps, "motivation to live is the mother of survival."

When we came back to the battalion area, we picked up a couple of the dead and wounded who tried to get us supplies the day before. We heard that one guy was riding on the "mule" hauling supplies; the others carelessly walked down the road and got ambushed.

We continued to man the company perimeter and saw more dead and wounded. I went by the aid station and saw that the second platoon leader of C Company was shot four times and killed. I identified with him and his death as I was second platoon leader of D Company.

I heard that a Medevac chopper was shot up, too. The NVA were dangerous, and I didn't like this area and hoped we all would get out alive. After a while, I got almost numb to the idea that I was mortal and could be killed at any time. I had been scared before but always did my best to hide it as I was the platoon leader and had to set the example.

In my view, if anyone has ever been in real combat and said he was never scared—he is simply a liar. My mind could keep me somewhat detached most of the time, but when I saw the 2nd platoon leader of C Company dead from being shot four times, I really personalized this. I was 2nd platoon leader of D company.

We didn't have any food or water all the previous day and for most of this day, and everyone was exhausted. Our mission to end the siege at Khe Sanh was not a cake walk!

On **April 5**, I got the word that our battalion (2/7 Cav) would head to Khe Sanh the next day. Based on everything I'd heard about Khe Sanh and what I had seen, I thought this could be disastrous. The Marines had been continuously shelled and surrounded by the NVA, but they were holding on.

The news reports made Khe Sanh appear to be an impending "Alamo," and the NVA were the "Mexicans." We had incurred a lot of dead and wounded since we had been there, and I had a lot of close calls. The NVA were numerous and good fighters, and everyone feared this area. As we dug in again for the night, jets kept circling the hill we occupied. There were a lot of choppers in the air, and artillery and bombing kept pounding nearby areas.

On **April 6**, we tried to walk from this LZ to Khe Sanh, but we had to come back because the two forward companies received effective fire, which slowed their advance. Our company was supposed to air assault to 500 meters east of Khe Sanh combat Base, and I thought that this was a glory push to see who could be the first to walk into Khe Sanh. I hoped we

Air Cavalry on an air assult to their objective during Operation Pegasus, 1968.

would make it because we had a lot of reporters with us. Although 1st Cavalry units relieved Marines at Hill 471 and airlifted Vietnamese Airborne into Khe Sanh Combat Base (KSCB), Route 9 still had to be cleared to the base.

On **April 7**, it was another unit's turn in the battalion to be the "point" in order of movement. We were supposed to be last in order of movement, and we thought we got a break, but the forward companies encountered NVA and were in a firefight. Our company was ordered to go back to the road to be picked up by chopper, leapfrog over the other companies, and continue the mission to clear Route 9. The Hueys came in two at a time, landed on the road (Route 9), and picked up my platoon.

We were ordered to lead the advance—to be the tip of the spear. It was common practice for commanders to rotate personnel or units as point elements for various reasons—one of which was to use the best people or unit to accomplish the mission. Of course, I thought we were the best in the company.

My platoon usually split up into groups (5 to 7 troops depending on equipment, number of troops, and missions), boarded the helicopters, and did air assaults, I was in the lead "chopper" with two of my

Captured NVA mortar rounds and arms.

RTOs, a M-60 machine-gunner, a "shot gunner," and riflemen.

We air assaulted near the top of a mountain that seemed to be solid rock, and my platoon was on point, again. As we approached the crest, I heard bullets whistle overhead. The ground had no cover and was too hard to dig in if we had to. We were on that laterite rock that Tolson later described in his memoirs.

We just kept moving toward the crest. We were out in the open with no opportunity for cover if fired on. We were wary as we moved forward when, up ahead of my position, the point squad radioed that they saw bunkers as they approached the crest.

The platoon was in an "on-line" formation so all firepower would be to the front as we expected a "firefight" any second, but nobody shot at us.

Eventually, we got to the crest, where we saw mounds of dirt around NVA fox-holes and fighting positions.

We crossed over the crest and came upon a deserted regimental-size NVA complex with commo wire linking bunkers surrounding the whole area. There were items of equipment and various weapons—mortars, machine guns, antiaircraft guns, ZPU-4s (4-barreled anti-craft guns), AKs, RPDs, RPKs (light machine-

Author photo.

NVA Bugle captured near Khe Sanh

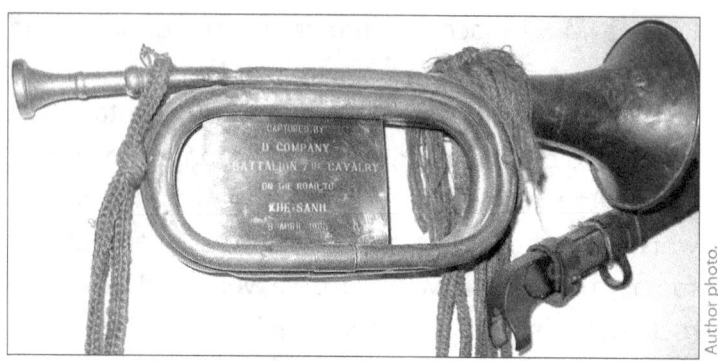

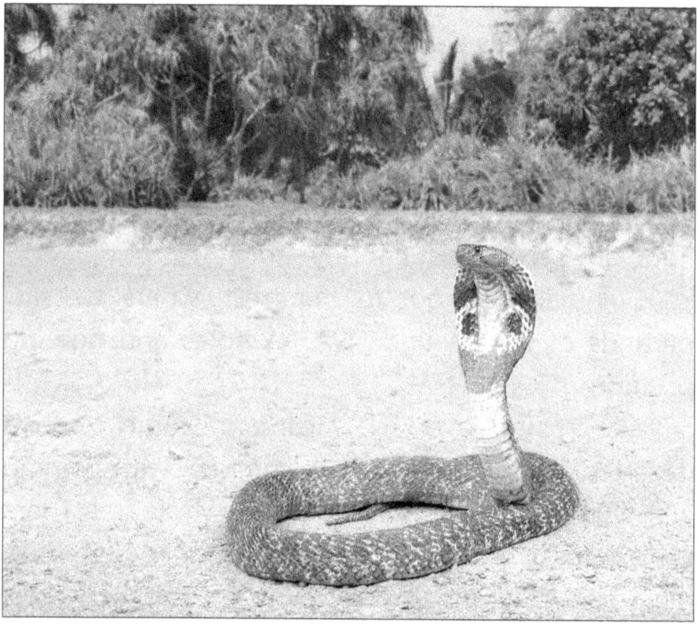

©Deposit Photos, Alinamd. Used with permission.

King Colbra

guns), RPGs (rocket propelled grenade launchers with ammo), hand grenades, mortars, and mortar rounds and other ammunition. We also found dead NVA soldiers in bunkers with blood coming out of their eyes, ears, and noses probably due to the bombing. The area was pockmarked with bomb craters courtesy of the U.S. Air Force and probably the result of Arc Lights (B-52 bombings). I love B-52s.

I got an AK-47, a NVA bayonet, and an ammo pouch as souvenirs, which I still have except for the AK—an issue for me later.

Turtle, in third squad, showed us a cobra stuck on an SKS rifle bayonet. It was a beautiful bluish-and-silver-color, pretty much shot up by a revolver he had. Turtle must have put all six rounds in the snake. He gave me the bugle he found, which is on display in the Arizona Military Museum.

We were about two miles outside of Khe Sanh Combat Base; and although this NVA bunker complex was abandoned, my platoon was tasked to lead the clearing action for the whole division for two miles of NVA, bunker-lined Route 9 leading to Khe Sanh.

We did not know the status of the NVA, as we cautiously proceeded along Route 9, avoiding "toe poppers" (small bomblets dropped by the Air Force) and other potential booby traps. We were aware that the NVA could still ambush us, so I had flank security (soldiers flanking their squads) straddle the road by 30 to 40 meters to avoid side ambushes. I kept the RTOs nearby for commo with my squads as I walked the road. Our weapons were "at the ready" because we did not know what awaited us, and we were concerned about being ambushed at any time by the NVA. This was Route 9—the road that the Marines could not move along for over two months.

As we "cleared the road," we found bunkers strategically placed lining the road all the way to the wire at Khe Sanh. No wonder the Marines were prevented from traversing up and down Route 9. We found NVA backpacks, opium, weapons, ammunition, etc.

Interestingly, the NVA had vanished. Some say that all the NVA left the area long before the Cavalry had come; but if they did, all they had to do was slip over the Laotian border and cross back and forth as they chose. Both of the borders of the DMZ to the north and Laos to the west were only a few "clicks" away.

General Tolson, the 1st Cavalry's Division commander, wrote in *"Vietnam Studies—Airmobility 1961-1971"* that the heaviest contact on April 6:

"... occurred in the 3d Brigade's area of operation as the 2d Battalion, 7th Cavalry, continued its drive west on Highway 9. In a daylong battle that ended when the enemy summarily abandoned his position and fled, the battalion had 83 NVA killed, one POW captured, and 121 individual and ten crew-served weapons captured. The 1st Cavalry Division troops were airlifted to Hill 471, relieving the Marines at this position. This was the first relief of the defenders of Khe Sanh.

Two companies of troopers remained on the hill while two other companies attacked to the south toward the Khe Sanh hamlet. The 1st Cavalry forces on landing zone Snapper were attacked by an enemy force using mortars, hand grenades, and rocket launchers. The attack was a disaster for the enemy, and twenty were killed.

The 84th Company of the Vietnamese 8th Airborne Battalion was airlifted by 1st Cavalry Division aircraft into Khe Sanh Combat Base and linked up with elements of the 37th Ranger Battalion. The lift was conducted without incident and was marked as the official link-up of forces at Khe Sanh."

Bernard C. Nalty / PD

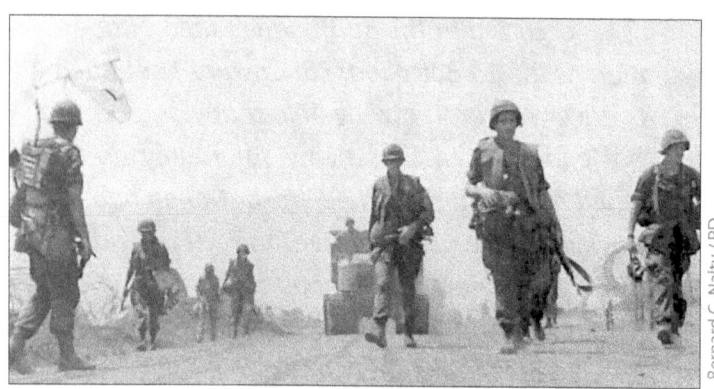

1st Cav troops entering Khe Sanh.

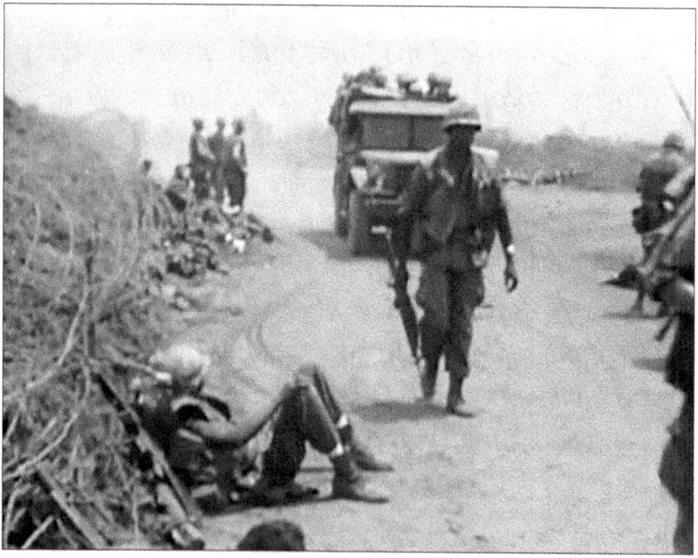

U.S. Army film clip. / PD

1st Air Cav enter Khe Sanh—Marines look on.

My diary entry:

"Sunday, April 7, 1700 hrs. We are at Khe Sanh camped outside the east entrance on Highway 9."

On **April 8**, the 2nd Battalion, 7th Cavalry Regiment of the 3rd Brigade entered the camp and linked up with the Marines at KSCB at 0800. My platoon (2nd platoon) was the tip of the spear of the 1st Air Cavalry Division relief force as we entered the wire perimeter at Khe Sanh, single file. My CO asked me if I could play the NVA bugle. I had played trumpet in junior high and first year of high school.

We entered Khe Sanh perimeter and walked single file toward the air control tower. I lead the column sounding the cavalry charge on the NVA bugle, with the M-16 in my left hand and AK-47 strapped across my back. We approached a Marine Captain, I halted the column, saluted, and said, "Sir, 2nd battalion, 7th Cavalry, 1st Air Cavalry reporting." He gave me the entire length of the airstrip to secure that night with just my platoon. *The Los Angeles Herald Examiner* reported:

"A two-mile victorious march by the Army 1st Air Cavalry Division formally ended the 78-day Communist siege at Khe Sanh, where round the

clock Communist artillery fire had driven 6,000 Marine defenders underground.

The Leathernecks Sunday whooped it up as Army 1st Lt. Joe Abodeely's unit walked the last two miles into the camp. Abodeely, 24, of Tucson, Ariz., and his platoon formed the 1st Air Cavalry spearhead of the 20,000-man Operation Pegasus drive that broke the Communist grip around Khe Sanh in a week-long drive that covered 12 miles of jungle, hills, and minefields.

The lieutenant triumphantly blew on the bugle he found in a captured arms dump. Abodeely's unit had landed by helicopter two miles from Khe Sanh and met no resistance the rest of the way..."

I made another diary entry:

"Today, D Company was the first to walk into Khe Sanh on Highway 9 in two months. My company—D, 2nd of the 7th Cav—was the lead unit.

This place is bunkers and trenches. The incoming artillery is deadly... Everything is in bunkers beneath the ground as the NVA continually shoots artillery here. The Marines have been pinned in but now they can move.

Newsmen, etc., were all around as we probably did something significant... This could be a turning point in the war. I hope all goes well. Anyway, we walked in on Highway 9, where no one before could travel because of ambushes. We cleared It."

I was ecstatic about our feat because the media made Khe Sanh seem like HELL! The Operation was an entire airmobile division (15,000 men) and ARVN and two Regiments of Marines. Much of the enemy fled as the Air Cav armada filled the sky.

As LTG Tolson reported:

"At 0800 on 8 April, the relief of Khe Sanh was effected and the 1st Cavalry Division became the new landlord. The 3d Brigade airlifted its command post into Khe Sanh...after the 2d Battalion, 7th Cavalry successfully cleared Highway 9 to the base and effected linkup with the 26th Marine Regiment."

Khe Sanh had strategic importance to prevent the NVA conquest of I Corps. After the war, I heard some Marines, who were never at Khe Sanh, claim Khe Sanh was not under "siege"—that the Marines could have fought their way out at any time—that the 1st Air Cav was never needed, but that misses the point because Khe Sanh had to be held due to its strategic location and importance. I later learned that a Marine "relief force" could not proceed down Route 9, and they got killed because the NVA controlled the area. Some Marines who were actually at Khe Sanh told me they were really glad to see the 1st Air Cav enter the perimeter wire.

After Khe Sanh, we went into the A Shau Valley and later operated along the coastal region ("The Street Without Joy").

After six months in the field, I was assigned various staff jobs including base defense sector commander for the battalion at Quan Loi before I came home in January 1969. Quan Loi was just up the road from An Loc where the NVA invaded Saigon in 1975.

2nd platoon D/2/7 Cavalry, 1st Cavalry Division (Airmobile).

Monday, APRIL 1

0817 We are waiting to be picked up to go to LZ Caloo. From there we go to LZ Thor. They have been decided definitely yet. The terrain there is thick and mountainous.

(Late entry) 20 Apr 0645 We air assaulted to the top of this mountain. It's jungle and grassy. I jumped from the chopper and shit my arms. At 2100 I could see bomb strikes off in the distance as the sky lit up and the ground shook.

Tuesday, APRIL 2

1000 The sun is out. We're on a high mountain top surrounded by a river on 3 sides. Today D company (mine) is to air assault to a new location to set up there. We just got a log ship with food and water. It was nice sleeping last night.

1720 D company led the air assault to where we are now. My plt. led a ground movement. We found a sight for 50 cal. anti aircraft gun. Also some of my plt found some ammo and grebades (NVA). Now we are waiting to see where we will set up. We're hot and tired.

Fire Insurance

0953   **Wednesday, APRIL 3**

We are sitting in the jungle right now. 3rd plt hit some NVA a little while ago. They got one of their men KIA. The S-2 carried him back on his shoulders and then 3 of my men took the KIA to the rear. We're waiting for artillery to come in. There are huge bomb craters all around. I can hear the choppers circling the area now. There are trees, high grass, and ferns all around.

1808 We moved to this hill – 242. NVA mortared us; we had 10 or 11 WIA. NVA have us surrounded. One plt from another company tried to bring us food and water but got pinned down. I hope we make it through the night. We dug in and made overhead cover.

Thursday, APRIL 4

1540 Last night we received more mortar and artillery fire. We are now back at the gpos.

1800 I have my plt in position on the perimeter. A lurk came back today. We picked up a couple of the dead and wounded who tried to get us supplies yesterday. When we got back here we saw more dead and wounded. The 2d plt ldr of C company was killed. One medivac chopper was shot up. The NVA here are dangerous. I don't like this area. I hope we all get out alive. I got a card from Colleen today which cheered me up. We didn't have any food or water all day yesterday and for most of today. Everyone is tired.

Vietnam Was A Just War

Friday, APRIL 5

9 1550 day. No wind
10. to lay off at our pos. We
 will walk to Khe Sanh
11 tomorrow. This could be disastrous.
 We've incurred alot of dead and
12 wounded since we've been here.
 I hope to God we make it alive.
1 I've had alot of close calls and
2 I'm getting scared again. Everyone
 is scared of Khe area. The NVA
3 are numerous and good fighters.
 We're digging in again for tonight.
4 1720 Jets keep circling skies. Artillery
5 flares are also alot of choppers in
 the air. Artillery kept pounding the
 surrounding area also. I hope the
 NVA move out. They ambush alot here.

Sat / Sun, APR 6-7

Sat 1400 Well, we tried to walk
from this LZ to Khe Sanh, but we had
to come back as the two forward
companies received effective fire. Now
our company is supposed to be air-assault
to 500 meters east of Khe Sanh.
This is a glory push to see who can
be the first to walk into Khe Sanh.
I hope we make it; we have many
reporters with us.

Sun 1045
We air assaulted to an open area on a
mountain top and received light sniper
fire. We found a complex (NVA) with
rockets, mortars - tube and ammo, AK-47s,
and all sorts of material. I have a
sharp AK-47 which I hope to keep. We
are to go to Khe Sanh.
1700 We are at Khe Sanh camp just outside the east entrance on Highway 9.

Joe Abodeely

Fijis in Viet Nam

JOSEPH ABODEELY
(Arizona '65)

Tucson, Ariz.) Army Lt. Joe Abodeely last Sunday led the first contingent of American relief forces into the beleaguered Marine camp at Khe Sanh Brother Abodeely, son of Mr. and Mrs. Ed Abodeely, 6039 E. 22nd St., has been with the Army's 1st Air Cavalry Division in Vietnam since Jan. 3.

Abodeely (Arizona '65), and his platoon formed the spearhead of the 20,000-man Operation Pegasus drive that broke the Cong noose about Khe Sanh in a week-long drive that covered 19 miles of jungle, hills and minefields.

Army and Marine forces approached the trapped Marines from three directions by helicopter leapfrog and roadway wedge movements. Abodeely's troops were lowered by chopper some two miles from the camp. They lunged toward Khe Sanh's barbed wire barriers--facing little resistance.

Abodeely, a graduate of Rincon High, was graduated from the University of Arizona in 1965.

Arizona DailyStar

Author's collection.

GIs Link Up at Khe Sanh, But Fight On

SAIGON (UPI) — Blowing "Charge!" on a captured Communist bugle, American ground forces linked up with the long-surrounded Marine fort of Khe Sanh and then fanned out and killed at least 103 North Vietnamese in the hills on South Vietnam's northern frontier, U.S. spokesmen said today.

A two-mile victorious march by the Army 1st Air Cavalry Division formally ended the 76-day Communist siege of the fort Hanoi vowed it would take and American generals pledged would never be lost.

The siege was over. But the battle for control of South Vietnam's Communist-infested northern frontier roared on. Besides the fighting in the hills near the fort, Leathernecks 25 miles southwest of the coastal city of Da Nang killed at least 68 Communists in a Sunday battle that cost no American casualties.

At Khe Sanh, where round-the-clock Communist artillery fire had driven 6000 Marines defenders underground, the Leathernecks Sunday whooped it up as Army 1st Lt. Joe Abodeely's unit walked the last two miles into the camp.

Abodeely, 24, of Tucson, Ariz. and his platoon formed the 1st Air Cavalry spearhead of the 20,000-man Operation Pegasus drive that broke the Communist grip around Khe Sanh in a week-long drive that covered 12 miles of jungle, hills and minefields.

The lieutenant triumphantly blew on the bugle he found in a captured arms dump. Its notes echoed across the red dirt plateau. Abodeely's unit had landed by helicopter two miles from Khe Sanh and met no resistance the rest of the way. The helicopter leapfrog technique, plus a Marine road-clearing drive, formed the backbone of Pegasus.

The payoff came when the lieutenant's men reached the barbed wire around the camp.

"Hey! We're here!" shouted Pfc. Juan Fordondi of Bay Amon, Puerto Rico. Marine Lance Cpl. James Hellebuick of Mount Clemens, Mich., whooped and from inside shoved a hand over the wire. GI Fordondi clasped it.

"We're really glad to see you guys," Hellebuick said, speaking for the defenders that for two days had seen relief only on the green hills of the horizon or on the landing strip where a token force of South Vietnamese paratroopers arrived Saturday.

The sudden collapse of Hanoi's might around Khe Sanh was seen in the trenches North Vietnamese troops had dug up to the fort's barbed wire defenses and then abandoned the past few days. In the trenches Abodeely's men found dozens of fresh field packs complete with Communist identification tags and clean uniforms.

Joe Abodeely

ARIZONA DAILY STAR APRIL 13, 1968

LT. JOE ABODEELY

Tucsonan Led Relief To Khe Sanh

Tucson Army Lt. Joe Abodeely last Sunday led the first contingent of American relief forces in to the beleaguered Marine camp at Khe Sanh.

Abodeely, son of Mr. and Mrs. Ed Abodeely, 6039 E. 22nd St., has been with the Army's 1st Air Cavalry Division in Vietnam since Jan. 3.

Abodeely, 24, and his platoon formed the spearhead of the 20,000-man Operation Pegasus drive that broke the Cong noose about Khe Sanh in a week-long drive that covered 12 miles of jungle, hills and minefields.

Army and Marine forces approached the trapped Marines from three directions by helicopter leapfrog and roadway wedge movements. Abodeely's troops were lowered by chopper some two miles from the camp. They lunged toward Khe Sanh's barbed wire barriers facing little resistance.

Abodeely, a graduate of Rincon High, was graduated from the University of Arizona in 1965.

★★★★ E
Des Moines Sunday Register
May 12, 1968
Third News Section 2-T

FORMER IOWAN AIDED KHE SANH

By William Simbro
(Register Staff Writer)

CEDAR RAPIDS, IA. — A former Cedar Rapids resident, Army Lt. Joe Abodeely, led the first contingent of American relief forces which last month lifted the Communist siege of Khe Sanh.

Abodeely, 24, and his platoon of men from the Army's 1st Air Cavalry Division, formed the spearhead of the 20,000-man Operation Pegasus drive that broke the noose about the Khe Sanh Marine base.

JOE ABODEELY

Abodeely is the son of Mr. and Mrs. Edward Abodeely, who moved from Cedar Rapids to Tucson, Ariz., several years ago. The lieutenant attended Coe College here and graduated from the University of Arizona in 1965.

His Cedar Rapids relatives include two cousins, Mrs. Dorothy Taylor and Mrs. George J. Homsey. Abodeely is a familiar name in Cedar Rapids, which has a sizeable Lebanese community.

TAMPA, FLA.
VIETNAM
REPORT ON THE WAR

'We're Glad To Be Here'

SAIGON (UPI) — Troops of the U.S. 1st Cavalry Division, sounding "charge" on a captured North Vietnamese bugle, walked the last two miles into Khe Sanh fortress yesterday and joined Marine defenders who had weathered the heaviest siege of the war.

"Hey, we're here!" Pfc. Juan Fordondi of Bay Amon, Puerto Rico, shouted to Lance Cpl. James Hellebuick of Mount Clemens, Mich., as the two men clasped hands over the Khe Sanh barbed wire.

"WE'RE REALLY glad to see you guys," Hellebuick replied for his 6,000 Marine buddies.

Lt. Joe Abodeely, 24, of Tucson, Ariz., reached through the wire, grabbed Hellebuick's hand and said: "We're glad to be here."

Abodeely blew a triumphant blast on the tarnished bugle he had found in a pile of abandoned North Vietnamese weapons along highway 9 as the air cavalrymen walked up the twisting narrow road and ended Operation Pegasus — the relief operation for Khe Sanh that began last Monday.

Although the linkup was the main objective of Pegasus, more fighting in the hills around Khe Sanh was reported between sweeping allied forces and diehard North Vietnamese dug into the high ground.

AN ESTIMATED 60 more North Vietnamese were killed as allied troops swept through the elephant grass and shell-scarred tea plantations surrounding Khe Sanh.

B52 stratofortresses struck two targets in the Khe Sanh area, blasting troop concentrations, bunkers and storage areas four and six miles southwest of the fortress.

WEDNESDAY, JANUARY 15, 1969
TUCSON DAILY CITIZEN

The Armed Services

Joseph Abodeely

FIRST LT. JOSEPH ABODEELY, son of Mr. and Mrs. Edward Abodeely, 6039 E. 22nd St., has been released from active duty with the Army after spending a year in Vietnam.

Abodeely, a graduate of Rincon High School and the University of Arizona, was awarded the Bronze Star and Air Medal for meritorious service in combat. He received the Air Medal while serving with the 1st Air Cavalry Division. He also was given Vietnamese service and campaign medals.

A rifle platoon leader for six months, Abodeely served with a company that initiated the campaign to relieve the encircled Marine camp at Khe Sanh.

Abodeely plans to take university graduate work. He served two years in the Army before being discharged early this month.

Khe Sanh news clippings of Joseph Abodeely.

Monday, April 8, 1968

1st Cavalry Bugles Way To Khe Sanh Marines

SAIGON (UPI) — Troops of the U.S. 1st Cavalry Division, sounding "charge" on a captured North Vietnamese bugle, walked the last two miles into Khe Sanh fortress Sunday and joined Marine defenders who had weathered the heaviest siege of the war.

"Hey, we're here!" Pfc. Juan Fordondi of Bay Amon, Puerto Rico, shouted to Lance Cpl. James Hellebuick of Mount Clements, Mich., as the two men clasped hands over the Khe Sanh barbed wire.

"WE'RE REALLY glad to see you guys," H e l l e b u i c k replied for his 6,000 Marines buddies.

Lt. Joe Abodeely, 24, of Tucson, Ariz., reached though the wire, grabbed Hellebuick's hand and said, "We're glad to be here."

Abodeely blew a triumphant blast on the tarnished bugle he had found in a pile of abandoned North Vietnamese weapons along Highway 9 as the air cavalrymen walked up the twisting narrow road and ended Operation Pegasus — the relief operation for Khe Sanh that began last Monday.

ALTHOUGH THE linkup was the main objective of Pegasus, more fighting in the hills around Khe Sanh was reported between sweeping allied forces and diehard North Vietnamese dug into the high ground.

UPI correspondent P e r r y Young, reporting late Sunday night from Khe Sanh, said troops of the 26th U.S. Marines and the 37th South Vietnamese Ranger Battalion had found about 100 North Vietnamese bodies killed by allied air and artillery south and east of Khe Sanh.

Young said 160 more North Vietnamese were killed during the 24 hours period ending at 6 p.m. Sunday as allied troops swept through the elephant grass and shell-scarred tea plantations surrounding Khe Sanh. In one fight, a Marine reconnaissance battalion battled a force of 100-200 Communists, and reported killing 68 without losing a man.

B-52 Stratofortresses struck two targets in the Khe Sanh area late Saturday and Sunday, blasting troop concentrations, bunkers and storage areas four and six miles southwest of the fortress.

OTHER B-52 flights struck just southeast of Khe Sanh in eight saturation m i s s i o n s against the A Shau Valley infiltration funnel from Laos into South Vietnam's northern provinces.

Three Accounts of Operation Pegasus

Lieutenant General John J. Tolson's History of Pegasus[1]

This, then, is how the situation stood in early 1968. Press correspondents began to dramatize the developments. Repeatedly the public was told that Khe Sanh was likely to be a "very rough business with heartbreaking American casualties." The impending battle was seen as a major test of strength between the U.S. and North Vietnam, with heavy political and psychological overtones.

On 2 March, I went to DA Nang to present our plan for the relief of Khe Sanh to General Cushman, Commanding General, III Marine Amphibious Force. In attendance at this briefing was General Abrams, Deputy Commander, U.S. Military Assistance Command, Vietnam, who still had his advance headquarters at

---

[1]. *Vietnam Studies*—Airmobility 1961-1971, Public Domain. See Credits.

Hue-Phu Bai. Our plan was approved in concept and provisional troop allocations were made.

To accomplish the mission, the 1st Cavalry Division would be augmented by the following non-divisional units: 1st Marine Regiment, 26th Marine Regiment, III Army of the Republic of Vietnam Airborne Task Force, and the 37th Army of the Republic of Vietnam Ranger Battalion. In all, I would have over 30,000 troops under my direct operational control.

Having been given the broad mission and the forces necessary, I was given complete freedom on how to do the job from the beginning. Seldom is a commander so blessed. In the early stages of planning, verbal orders were the modus operandi. As the concept took shape, I asked for representatives from all the units that would be working with us and detailed plans were developed under the critical supervision of Colonel Putnam. We even constructed a sand table model of the Khe Sanh area. I made several trips into the surrounded Marine garrison to coordinate directly with its commander, Colonel David E. Lownds.

Many different elements were involved and all would have to be pulled together under my command on D-day. If we wanted surprise, speed and flexibility during the actual attack, everyone had to understand their part of the plan and the control procedures. This was especially true of firepower. A lot of things were going to be moving through the same air space—bombs, rockets, artillery shells, helicopters and airplanes. We had to assure ourselves that none got together inadvertently.

The basic concept of Operation PEGASUS was as follows: The 1st Marine Regiment with two battalions would launch a ground attack west toward Khe Sanh while the 3d Brigade would lead the 1st Cavalry air assault.

On D+1 and D+2 all elements would continue to attack west toward Khe Sanh; and, on the following day, the 2d Brigade of the Cavalry would land three battalions southeast of Khe Sanh and attack northwest. The 26th Marine Regiment, which was holding Khe Sanh, would attack south to secure Hill 471. On D+4, the 1st Brigade would air assault just south of Khe Sanh and attack north.

The following day the 3d Army of the Republic of Vietnam Airborne Task Force would air assault southwest of Khe Sanh and attack toward Lang Vei Special Forces Camp. Linkup was planned at the end of seven days.

It became evident during the planning that the

construction of an airstrip in the vicinity of Ca Lu would be a key factor for the entire operation. This airstrip, which became known as landing zone STUD, had to be ready well before D-day (I April, 1968). Also, it was necessary to upgrade Highway 9 between the "Rock Pile" and Ca Lu to allow pre-stocking of supplies at landing zone STUD.

I sent one of my assistant division commanders, Brigadier General Oscar E. Davis, to personally supervise the establishing of landing zone STUD as our advance base for PEGASUS. Calling this a "landing zone" is a gross understatement, for landing zone STUD would have to be a major air terminal, communications center, and supply depot for the future. The 1st Cavalry Division engineers, the Seabees USN Mobile Construction Battalion 5, and the 11th Engineer Battalion did the work.

In order to correct an impression given by the newsreel coverage at this time, I must point out that the only "safe" way to get into the Khe Sanh Combat Base was by helicopter. I usually chose to land in the Special Forces area. The C-130's were either delivering their loads by low altitude extraction or by parachute. The runway was the most dangerous and exposed area at Khe Sanh.

USMC initiated construction of the C-7A airfield and parking ramp, logistical facilities, and a bunker complex at landing zone STUD on 14 March. By D-6 they had finished an airstrip 1500 feet long by 600 feet wide, ammunition storage areas, aircraft and vehicle refueling facilities, and extensive road nets into the vicinity of landing zone STUD. The Seabees, which had been augmented with very heavy equipment, accomplished the lion's share of the work on the airfield.

Having established a forward base of operations, the second key element to the success of this plan was the tightly integrated reconnaissance and fire support effort of the 1st Squadron, 9th Cavalry, under the brilliant leadership of Lieutenant Colonel Richard W. Diller, and air, artillery, and B-52 Arc Light strikes, during the period D-6 to D-day. This was almost a flawless demonstration of properly preparing a battlefield when tactical intelligence was not available. This is not to say there was not a tremendous intelligence effort focused around Khe Sanh Combat Base, itself.

In addition to the aerial observation and daily photographic coverage, General Westmoreland had personally made the decision to divert new acoustic sensors from their intended emplacement along the DMZ to the approaches around Khe Sanh.

Through a complex computer system, these devices could provide early warning of any intrusion and were often used to target B-52 strikes. However, the acoustical sensor system, which was focused on the immediate area of Khe Sanh, did not directly help develop the complete intelligence picture necessary for our proposed attack along Highway Nine.

The actual intelligence on the enemy in the area was very vague and expressed in generalities. The 1st Squadron, 9th Cavalry operated from landing zone STUD in gradually increasing concentric circles up to the Khe Sanh area, working all the time with aircover from the 7th Air Force or the 1st Marine Air Wing. The Cavalry Squadron was almost the only means available to pinpoint enemy locations, antiaircraft positions, and strong points that the division would try to avoid in the initial assaults. The squadron was also responsible for the selection of critical landing zones. Their information proved to be timely and accurate.

During the initial surveillance efforts, it became evident that the enemy had established positions designed to delay or stop any attempt to reinforce or relieve Khe Sanh. Positions were identified on key terrain features both north and south of Highway Nine. As part of the reconnaissance by fire, known or suspected enemy antiaircraft positions and troop concentrations were sought out and destroyed either by organic fire or tactical air.

Landing zones were selected and preparations of the landing zones for future use were accomplished by tactical air using specially fused bombs and B-52 Arc Light strikes. During this phase of the operation, the 1st Squadron, 9th Cavalry developed targets for 632 sorties of tactical air, 49 sorties for the specially fused bombs, and twelve B-52 Arc Light strikes. The thoroughness of the battlefield preparation was demonstrated during the initial assaults of the 1st Cavalry Division, for no aircraft were lost due to antiaircraft fire or enemy artillery.

At this point, I must mention the element of surprise. Certainly, the enemy knew we were in the area. Our own reporters let the whole world know the situation as they saw it, and the arm-chair strategist could ponder the problem each evening in front of his color TV. However, the inherent capabilities of the airmobile division presented the enemy with a bewildering number of possible thrusts that he would have to counter, all the way to the Laotian border. Also, there would be a major diversionary attack in the vicinity of the DMZ on D-1. The initiative was ours.

At 0700 on 1 April, 1968, the attack phase of Operation PEGASUS commenced as two battalions of the 1st Marine Regiment under Colonel Stanley S. Hughes attacked west from Ca Lu along Highway Nine. The 11th Marine Engineers followed right on their heels. At the same time, the 3d Brigade of the 1st Cavalry under Colonel Hubert (Bill) S. Campbell was airlifted by Chinooks and Hueys into landing zone STUD in preparation for an air assault into two objective areas further west. Weather delayed the attack until 1300, when the 1st Battalion, 7th Cavalry, commanded by Lieutenant Colonel Joseph E. Wasiak, air assaulted into landing zone MIKE located on prominent ground south of Highway Nine and well forward of the Marine attack.

Lieutenant Colonel Roscoe Robinson, Jr., led the 2nd Battalion, 7th Cavalry into the same landing zone to expand and develop the position. The 5th Battalion, 7th Cavalry, commanded by Lieutenant Colonel James B. Vaught, air assaulted into an area north of Highway Nine approximately opposite landing zone MIKE. These two objectives had been chosen after careful reconnaissance by the Cavalry Squadron indicated no major enemy defenses. Though almost halfway to Khe Sanh, they were within range of supporting artillery.

Both landing zones were secured and no significant enemy resistance was encountered.

A battery of 105-mm howitzers was airlifted into each landing zone and Colonel Campbell moved his brigade headquarters into the northern landing zone, landing zone CATES. Bad weather notwithstanding, everything was in place prior to darkness. The major accomplishment of D-day was the professional manner in which this tremendously complex operation, with all its split-second timing and coordination, had to be delayed several hours yet was completed as planned.

The bad weather of D-day was to haunt the 1st Cavalry throughout Operation PEGASUS. Seldom were airmobile moves feasible much before 1300. "Good weather" was considered to be any condition when the ceiling was above 500 feet and slant range visibility was more than a mile and a half. The bad weather further proved the soundness of establishing landing zone STUD as the springboard for the assaults. Troops, ammo and supplies could be assembled there ready to go whenever the weather to the west opened up. Marshalling areas further away would have drastically deteriorated response time.

On D+1 (2 April), the 1st Marine Regiment continued its ground attack along the axis of Highway Nine.

Two Marine companies made limited air assaults to support the Regiment's momentum. The 3d Brigade air assaulted the 2d Battalion, 7th Cavalry into a new position further to the west while the other two battalions improved their positions. The 2d Brigade under Colonel Joseph C. McDonough moved into marshalling areas in preparation for air assaults the next day, if called upon.

Lest all of this sound routine, I want to emphasize that only the initial assaults on D-day were fixed in time or place. All subsequent attacks were varied to meet changes in the enemy situation or to capitalize on unexpected progress. As an example, I ordered an acceleration of the tempo when the results of D-day attacks gave clear evidence that the enemy was unprepared.

Our initial thrusts had met less enemy resistance than expected. As a consequence, the 2d Brigade was thrown into the attack a day earlier than the original schedule with three battalions moving into two new areas south and west of our earlier landing zones. They received enemy artillery during the assaults but secured their objectives without serious difficulty. We now had six air cavalry battalions and supporting artillery deep in enemy territory.

I was anxious to get the 26th Marine Regiment out of their static defense position as soon as feasible; so, on D+3, I ordered Colonel Lownds to make a battalion-size attack south from Khe Sanh to seize Hill 471, a strategic piece of terrain affording a commanding view of the base. Following a heavy artillery preparation, the Marines successfully seized the hill killing thirty of the enemy. On the same day, the 2d Brigade of the Cavalry Division assaulted one battalion into an old French fort south of Khe Sanh. Initial contact resulted in four enemy killed. The remaining uncommitted brigade was moved into marshalling areas.

On D+4 (5 April), the 2d Brigade continued its attack on the old French fort meeting heavy enemy resistance. Enemy troops attacked the Marines on Hill 471 but were gallantly repulsed with 122 of the enemy left dead on the battlefield. The tempo of this battle was one of the heaviest during the operation. The 3d Airborne Task Force, Army of the Republic of Vietnam, was alerted to prepare to airlift one rifle company from Quang Tri to effect linkup with the 37th Army of the Republic of Vietnam Ranger Battalion located at Khe Sanh. Units of the 1st Brigade under Colonel Stannard entered the operation with the 1st Battalion, 8th Cavalry, commanded by Lieutenant Colonel Christian

F. Dubia, air assaulting into landing zone SNAPPER, due south of Khe Sanh and overlooking Highway Nine. The circle began to close around the enemy.

On D+5 (6 April), the 1st Marine Regiment continued its operations on the high ground north and south of Highway Nine, moving to the west toward Khe Sanh. The heaviest contact on that date occurred in the 3d Brigade's area of operation as the 2d Battalion, 7th Cavalry under the inspired leadership of Colonel Robinson continued its drive west on Highway Nine. Enemy blocking along the highway offered stubborn resistance.

In a day-long battle that ended when the enemy summarily abandoned his position and fled, the battalion had accounted for 83 enemy killed, one prisoner of war captured, and 121 individual and ten crew-served weapons captured. The troops of the 1st Cavalry Division were airlifted to Hill 471 relieving the Marines at this position. This was the first relief of the defenders of Khe Sanh. Two companies of troopers remained on the hill while two other companies initiated an attack to the south toward the Khe Sanh Hamlet.

We had plotted heavy enemy artillery that had been dug deeply into the rocks of the Co Roc Mountains in Laos just west of Lang Vei. As we neared Khe Sanh, I was concerned that these 152-mm guns could bring our landing zones under fire at any time. But we were forbidden to cross the border and the heaviest aerial bombs could not dislodge these positions. They remained a threat throughout PEGASUS.

The 1st Cavalry forces on landing zone SNAPPER were attacked by an enemy force utilizing mortars, hand grenades, and rocket launchers. The attack was a disaster for the enemy and twenty were killed. At 1320 the 84th Company of the Vietnamese 8th Airborne Battalion was airlifted by 1st Cavalry Division aircraft into the Khe Sanh Combat Base and linked up with elements of the 37th Ranger Battalion. The lift was conducted without incident and was marked as the official link-up in forces at Khe Sanh.

On 7 April, the South Vietnamese III Airborne Task Force air assaulted three battalions into positions north of the road and east of Khe Sanh to block escape routes toward the Laotian border. Fighting throughout the area was sporadic as the enemy attempted to withdraw. American and South Vietnamese units began picking up significant quantities of abandoned weapons and equipment. The old French fort which was the last known enemy strong point around Khe Sanh was completely secured.

At 0800 on 8 April, the relief of Khe Sanh was effected and the 1st Cavalry Division became the new landlord. The 3d Brigade airlifted its command post into Khe Sanh and Colonel Campbell assumed the mission of securing the area.

This was accomplished after the 2d Battalion, 7th Cavalry successfully cleared Highway Nine to the base and effected linkup with the 26th Marine Regiment. The 3d Brigade elements occupied high ground to the east and northeast of the base with no enemy contact. At this time, it became increasingly evident, through lack of contact and the large amounts of new equipment being found indiscriminately abandoned on the battlefield, that the enemy had fled the area rather than face certain defeat. He was totally confused by the swift, bold, many-pronged attacks. Operations continued to the west.

On 9 April, all 1st Marine Regiment objectives had been secured and Highway Nine was repaired and secured with only scattered incidents of enemy sniper fires. Enemy mortar, rocket and artillery fire into Khe Sanh became increasingly sporadic.

On the following day, the 1st Battalion of the 12th Cavalry, commanded by Lieutenant Colonel Robert C. Kerner, under the 1st Brigade seized the old Lang

Vei Special Forces Camp four miles west of Khe Sanh against light enemy resistance.

This was the site of an enemy attack in mid-February when North Vietnamese troops, supported by armor, overran the camp. Early on the 10th, a helicopter from A Troop, 1st Squadron, 9th Cavalry, had located a PT-76 tank and had called in a tactical airstrike on the vehicle. The tank was destroyed along with fifteen enemy troops.

Though this was the only recorded tank kill during Operation PEGASUS, we had had intelligence of enemy armor throughout this area. The enemy's offensive at Lang Vei Special Forces Camp had given undeniable proof of this enemy capability and, since that time, intelligence sources estimated a possible company-size armor unit near Khe Sanh.

The 1st Squadron, 9th Cavalry had sighted tank treads several times in their early reconnaissance before D-day. Before the operation, I had directed the division to be prepared to use the SS-11 missile system during PEGASUS. This system, which employed a wire-guided armor-piercing missile had been in the theater since the arrival of the 1st Cavalry. However, the lack of lucrative targets had reduced its usefulness.

The system had been standardized in the U.S.

Army since 1960 when it replaced the lighter French SS-10 missile. Since then, hundreds of gunners had been trained at Fort Rucker, Alabama, in the use of the SS-11. We were never able to target this system during PEGASUS, but I still felt it was a valuable capability that should be maintained in constant readiness.

Highway Nine into the Khe Sanh Combat Base was officially opened on 11 April after the Marine engineers had worked day and night to complete their task. In eleven days, the engineers had reconstructed over fourteen kilometers of road, repaired or replaced nine bridges, and constructed seventeen bypasses. Numerous sections of the road had to be cleared of landslides and craters.

I had scheduled more than 38 additional operations to extend our control of Khe Sanh area but, without warning, on the morning of 10 April I received orders from General Rosson to make plans to extract the Division as soon as possible to prepare for an assault into the A Shau Valley. Advance units started pulling out on the 11th. Limited operations continued until 15 April when Operation PEGASUS was officially terminated.

There was great potential for the continued air assault operations that were abruptly closed. The enemy was vulnerable; he was abandoning his equipment; and he was completely disorganized. The decision to expedite our withdrawal immediately upon completing our primary mission-the relief of Khe Sanh Combat Base-was predicated on a long-range forecast which predicted April as the last possible time for air assault operations in the A Shau Valley before the heavy monsoon rains.

Operation PEGASUS-LAM SON 207A from its inception to its final extraction from the area of operations will long stand as a classic example of airmobile operations. The operation dramatically illustrated the speed and effectiveness with which a large force can be employed in combat using airmobile tactics and techniques.

The enemy's repeated failure to quickly comprehend the quick reaction time and capabilities of the 1st Cavalry Division led to his defeat, forced withdrawal, and eventual rout from the battlefield. The enemy was helpless and confused, suffered great losses of men and equipment, and failed in his mission to block and delay the relief of Khe Sanh.

No summation of Operation PEGASUS would be complete without mention of the great team effort of all the Services-Army, Navy, Marines and Air Force.

The operation was an ideal example of the synchronization of massive B-52 strikes, tactical air support and artillery firepower with ground maneuver. The South Vietnamese troops gave a splendid performance.

The fact that we were able to co-ordinate all of these operations in a single headquarters was a commander's dream. There was no question of command or who was calling the signals. Equally important, I had the full support of General Rosson, who commanded the Provisional Corps Vietnam, and of General Cushman, Commanding General, III Marine Amphibious Force.

The success of the PEGASUS operation can largely be attributed to the detailed planning and preparation that occurred prior to D-day and the effective reconnaissance and surveillance of the area of operations provided by the air cavalry squadron. This reconnaissance and its ability to develop hard targets for the tactical air and B-52 Arc Light strikes cannot be overestimated.

The concept of building landing zone STUD as a pivot point for the entire operation proved sound. This base provided a continuous flow of needed supplies and equipment to forward elements of the division. The success of the initial battalion air assaults was rapidly exploited by aggressive company and even platoon-size air assaults, all supported by artillery and air. The enemy, although well dug in, well supplied, and with an initial determination to deter the relief of Khe Sanh, found himself surrounded with no choice but to retreat in rout order back into Laos, leaving behind 1,304 dead and much valuable equipment strewn over the battlefield.

The total success of the operation can be best measured by the mission accomplished. For the first time, the Cavalry had made an air assault as a division entity; every committed battalion came into combat by helicopter.

In fifteen days, the division had entered the area of operations, defeated the enemy, relieved Khe Sanh, and been extracted from the assault-only to assault again in four days into the heart of the North Vietnamese Army's bastion in the A Shau Valley.

Wikipedia—Battle of Khe Sanh[2]

Although Westmoreland's planned relief effort infuriated the Marines, who had not wanted to hold Khe Sanh, and General Cushman was appalled by the implication of a rescue by outside forces, the Wikipedia "analysis" portrays Marines as patrolling freely outside the base prior

2. Excerpted from Wikipedia. See Credits.

to the 1st Cavalry's arrival. The relief troops were the 1st Cavalry Division (15,000 troops), ARVNs, and a couple of Marine battalions. The Marines were often decimated when they left the perimeter, so Westmoreland ordered them to stay within the perimeter wire during the 77 days of siege until Operation PEGASUS concluded. Wikipedia's account follows:

The Battle of Khe Sanh (January 21–July 9, 1968) was in the Khe Sanh area of northwestern Quang Tri Province, Republic of Vietnam (South Vietnam). The main US forces defending Khe Sanh Combat Base (KSCB) were two regiments of the United States Marine Corps supported by elements from the United States Army and the United States Air Force (USAF), as well as a small number of Army of the Republic of Vietnam (ARVN) troops. They faced two to three divisions of the North Vietnamese Army.

The US command in Saigon initially believed that combat operations around KSCB during 1967 were part of a series of minor NVA offensives in the border regions. That appraisal was later altered when the NVA was found to be moving major forces into the area. US forces were built up before the NVA isolated the Marine base. A series of actions was fought over a period of five months once the base came under siege. During this time, KSCB and the hilltop outposts around it were subjected to constant NVA artillery, mortar, and rocket attacks, and several infantry assaults.

A massive aerial bombardment campaign (Operation Niagara) was launched by the USAF to support the Marine base as over 100,000 tons of bombs were dropped by US aircraft and over 158,000 artillery rounds were fired in defense of the base. Throughout the campaign, US forces used the latest technology to locate NVA forces for targeting. Additionally, the logistical effort required to support the base once it was isolated demanded the implementation of other tactical innovations to keep the Marines supplied.

In March 1968, an overland relief expedition (Operation Pegasus) was launched by a combined Marine–Army/ARVN task force that eventually broke through to the Marines at Khe Sanh. American commanders considered the defense of Khe Sanh a success but, shortly after the siege was lifted, the decision was made to dismantle the base rather than risk similar battles in the future.

On June 19, the evacuation and destruction of KSCB began. Amid heavy shelling, the Marines attempted to salvage what they could before destroying what remained as they were evacuated. Minor attacks continued before the base was officially closed on July 5. Marines remained around Hill 689, though, and fighting in the vicinity continued until July 11 until they were finally withdrawn, bringing the battle to a close.

In the aftermath, the North Vietnamese proclaimed a victory at Khe Sanh, while US forces claimed that they had withdrawn because the base was no longer required. Historians have observed that the Battle of Khe Sanh may have distracted American and South Vietnamese attention from the buildup of Viet Cong (VC) forces in the south before the early 1968 Tet Offensive. Nevertheless, the US commander during the battle, General William Westmoreland, maintained that the true intention of Tet was to distract forces from Khe Sanh. . . .

Operation Pegasus (April 1–14, 1968) Planning for the overland relief of Khe Sanh had begun as early as January 25, 1968 when Westmoreland ordered General John J. Tolson, commander, First Cavalry Division, to prepare a contingency plan. Route 9, the only practical overland route from the east, was impassable due to its poor state of repair and the presence of PAVN troops. Tolson was not happy with the assignment, since he believed that the best course of action, after

Tet, was to use his division in an attack into the A Shau Valley. Westmoreland, however, was already planning ahead. Khe Sanh would be relieved and then used as the jump-off point for a "hot pursuit" of enemy forces into Laos.

On 2 March, Tolson laid out what became known as Operation Pegasus, the operational plan for what was to become the largest operation launched by III MAF thus far in the conflict. The 2nd Battalion, 1st Marine Regiment (2/1 Marines) and the 2/3 would launch a ground assault from Ca Lu Combat Base (16 km east of Khe Sanh) and head west on Route 9 while the 1st, 2nd, and 3rd Brigades of the 1st Cavalry Division, would air-assault key terrain features along Route 9 to establish fire support bases and cover the Marine advance.

The advance would be supported by 102 pieces of artillery. The Marines would be accompanied by their 11th Engineer Battalion, which would repair the road as the advance moved forward. Later, the 1/1 Marines and 3rd ARVN Airborne Task Force (the 3rd, 6th, and 8th Airborne Battalions) would join the operation.

Westmoreland's planned relief effort infuriated the Marines, who had not wanted to hold Khe Sanh in the first place and who had been roundly criticized for not defending it well. The Marines had constantly argued that technically, Khe Sanh had never been under siege since it had never truly been isolated from resupply or reinforcement. Cushman was appalled by the implication of a rescue or breaking of the siege by outside forces.

Regardless, on April 1, Operation Pegasus began. Opposition from the North Vietnamese was light and the primary problem that hampered the advance was continual heavy morning cloud cover that slowed the pace of helicopter operations. As the relief force made progress, the Marines at Khe Sanh moved out from their positions and began patrolling at greater distances from the base. Things heated up for the air cavalrymen on April 6 when the 3rd Brigade encountered a NVA blocking force and fought a day-long engagement.

On the following day, the 2nd Brigade of the 1st Air Cavalry captured the old French fort near Khe Sanh village after a three-day battle. The link-up between the relief force and the Marines at KSCB took place at 0800 on April 8, when the 2nd Battalion, 7th Cavalry Regiment entered the camp. The 11th Engineers proclaimed Route 9 open to traffic on April 11. On that day, Tolson ordered his unit to immediately prepare for Operation Delaware, an air assault into the A Shau Valley. At 0800 on April 15, Operation Pegasus was officially terminated.

Total US casualties during the operation were 92 killed, 667 wounded, and five missing. Thirty-three ARVN troops were also killed and 187 were wounded. Because of the close proximity of the enemy and their high concentration, the massive B-52 bombings, tactical airstrikes, and vast use of artillery, NVA casualties were estimated by MACV as being between 10,000 and 15,000 men.

On April 15, Operation Pegasus ended, and the 3rd Marine Division resumed responsibility for KSCB.

The National Vietnam War Museum

The following is on the website for the National Vietnam War Museum in Texas:

"The National Vietnam War Museum project was formalized in 1998 to develop a national venue that would create an atmosphere of learning about the Vietnam War era and engage people of all ages, nationalities, and political points of view."

I received solicitation mail, postmarked 4/26/22, requesting financial support for the National Vietnam War Museum. The article about Khe Sanh caught my interest, and I was astonished about the slanted version of the relief of Khe Sanh narrative since I know something about it.

The narrative was titled "Remembering the Siege of Khe Sanh." It described the actions of the base commander, Colonel Lownds, directing his Marines on Hill 881N to pull back to the hill south of them for a better defensive position for the pending attack which occurred on January 21, 1968.

The author further described the battle as hundreds of rockets, mortars, and artillery pounded Khe Sanh, and a rocket hit the ammo dump. Explosions occurred for the next 48 hours causing deaths and injuries to the Marines. All that was correct.

On nearby Hill 861, NVA attacked and breached the perimeter. The Marines regained control in a counterattack. Resupply of the base was by C-130 and C-123 aircraft. Tactical aircraft made corridors for safe resupply by air by helicopters. Over a two-month period B-52 bombers from Guam and Thailand dropped 100,000 to 150,000 tons of explosives. All of that was correct.

Then, the narrative proclaimed that the siege was lifted, but it did not say **HOW** that occurred. ***There was no mention that Operation Pegasus***—that the 1st Air Cavalry ended the siege in a 20,000-man, week-long drive to clear Route 9, the route to Khe Sanh Combat Base. ***This is another example of misrepresentation by omission.***

Misrepresentation of relevant facts by omission about the Vietnam War is unconscionable; but some historians and pseudo-historians, with a bias, or out of ignorance will distort "historical facts." I support museums and history if they are accurate. Slanted history is a disservice to those who want to learn the lessons of history.

"Those who cannot remember the past, are condemned to repeat it." ~ George Santayana

The Orthodox Versus the Revisionists

Why Is the Vietnam War Still Misrepresented?

The U.S. media whitewashed the precipitous withdrawal from Afghanistan, but it defamed the Vietnam War, which the U.S. military initially left as "victors." U.S. actions in Iraq and Afghanistan are instructive for comparison to U.S. involvement in Vietnam to give credit where credit is due to Vietnam veterans. The times change attitudes.

The U.S. invasion of Iraq was questionable and based on duplicity and greediness because there were no weapons of mass destruction, and the Saudis actually bombed the World Trade Center. Yet, the U.S. and its allies killed thousands of innocent Iraqis. If the Court had jurisdiction over U.S. combatants, U.S. troops and military leaders could be "defendants" before the International Criminal Court hearing cases involving war crimes committed by the U.S.

The U.S. occupation of Afghanistan lasted long after the mission to kill bin Laden. The precipitous withdrawal was a fiasco, and innocent civilians were killed due to U.S. incompetence. The Afghanistan fighters prevailed after the U.S. exit.

Attitudes change about the nature, reasons, conduct, and the criteria for service in war—but attitudes have not really changed about the Vietnam War and those who served in it. President Nixon wanted "peace with honor," but he got caught in a third-rate eavesdropping case (Watergate) which a liberal, Democrat Congress and antiwar groups used to defame him, the war, and those who served in Vietnam.

Academia rarely presented studies about the Vietnam War in high school or college although its study is still relevant and of interest to those who study history and the military, but *a fundamental problem studying any war is the blind acceptance of uniformed, false, or prejudicial views about the war.* There is no real counter to "fake news" about Vietnam.

Books, literature, museums, academia, and movies, still omit meaningful Vietnam War history while numerous pseudo-military historians wrote books about the Vietnam War and showed their ignorance of the geopolitics, tactics, and other dynamics of the war. They stuck to the "party line"—that the war was "illegal," that "America should not have been involved," that

U.S. "servicemen were war criminals," and that America "lost the war"—*all false*.

"Fake news" is not a new phenomenon. Fake news was good business during the Vietnam War years as the media, academia, and Congress, influenced by the antiwar disinformation about the war, was rampant and uncontradicted. The so-called "peace movement" took over college campuses, burned ROTC buildings, incited riots and violence, demoralized combat veterans, prolonged the war, contributed to reeducation camps for the Vietnamese, created boat people, and story-lines for a biased media. Ken Burns' propaganda—his so-called documentary about Vietnam—validated the antics of the antiwar crowd who were portrayed as the "good guys" while Vietnam veterans were the "bad guys."

As early as 1951, South Vietnamese and American advisors were defending themselves against Communist Viet Cong attacks in Vietnam. In 1954, the United States and other countries formed SEATO—the Southeast Asia Treaty Organization—to prevent communism from gaining ground in the region.

In 1964, the Gulf of Tonkin incident involved VC gunboats firing on a U.S. destroyer. Communist Viet Cong and North Vietnamese Army forces invaded

South Vietnam in violation of the international treaty (SEATO).

U.S. involvement increased, and it sent the 1st Cavalry Division and two Marine battalions to Vietnam in 1965. The war raged on, and the U.S. was successful in actions against the NVA, winning all the conflicts in over two decades of fighting.

In 1973, the Paris Peace Accords ended the war and provided that U.S. POWs were to be returned; the U.S. and all warring parties were to leave; South Vietnam was to hold free elections.

But the Viet Cong in the South never left, and they renewed aggression against the South Vietnamese; therefore, free elections could not be held. The U.S. agreed to resupply the South with replacement ammunition, fuel, and equipment as needed if the Communists renewed aggression, but *the Democrat Congress cut off all the funding* for resupply to the South Vietnamese allies. South Vietnam literally ran out of ammunition, artillery rounds, aircraft fuel, equipment spare parts, etc. The South Vietnamese fought as long as they could; but U.S. betrayal sealed their fate.

Vietnam veterans' service was extraordinary as they won all their major battles before leaving Vietnam in 1973. The average infantryman in Vietnam served 240 days in combat in one year while the average infantryman in WW II served about 40 days in actual combat in four years. Two-thirds who served in Vietnam volunteered as opposed to one-third in WW II who volunteered. WW II ended with nuclear devices being dropped and decades of U.S. rebuilding damaged countries. Unlike WW II, the U.S. military returned home from Vietnam to a hostile home front.

Those who served in Vietnam risked their lives and limbs in the defense of South Vietnam as part of their duty, while Congress, the media, and the protesters defamed them.

Congress threw away what they had won. There is a saying to the effect that the history of wars is written by the victors. The unprincipled "victors of the Vietnam War" were the U.S. media, academia, Communist sympathizers, the Democrat Congress, and the draft dodgers. When I associate with my Vietnamese friends, I am amazed by how well they overcame the trauma and tragedy of the loss of their country. Many were the "boat-people" braving the ocean, pirates, murder, rape, and thuggery. Now, their progeny are educated and hard-working members of society.

I understand what the people in Ukraine are experiencing because I have seen the horror on the faces of people whose country was ravaged and fear on those who face death. I know the terror of being in the combat zone, never knowing when I may meet eternity. The Ukrainians simply want help defending their homeland from the Russian aggressors just as South Vietnam wanted help defending against the NVA and VC.

The Vietnam War will probably remain controversial for a few more years and then be totally dismissed from human thought except to be ignorantly cited as a synonym for "failure" or "fiasco," although the U.S. military won; and the rest of America threw it all away. The Vietnam War was a "just war." It was a year of living dangerously for me.

The Vietnam War was simply the politics of the times; as Carl von Clausewitz said, "War is nothing but a continuation of politics with the admixture of other means." Unfortunately, domestic politics turned against its own whom they sent to war.

An ancient Greek philosopher, Heraclitus (circa 500 B.C.) opined:

> *"In war, every one-hundred men, ten should not even be there, eighty are nothing but targets, nine are real fighters, ...we are lucky to have*

them… they make the battle. Ah, but the One, one of them is a warrior… and He will bring the others back."

All of those who served were truly heroes and won the war before they left in 1973. I am proud to say that I served with those "heroes," and by luck, skill, or by Divine Providence, I never lost a man who served under my command in combat. I am proud of that.

To those who served in Vietnam, came home, became productive members of society, and have tried to understand the meaning of "Vietnam"—WELCOME HOME!

Vietnam Anti-War Movement

It is impossible to talk about the Vietnam War without addressing the *antiwar movement* which was really *several combined movements*. Numerous U.S. domestic events illustrated *the counter-culture which maligned our U.S. service personnel* in the Vietnam War. The times were crazy. While young men *served their country, fighting and dying* in the jungles of South Vietnam, antiwar protests occurred in the United States and elsewhere. Those who were subject to the draft were terrified.

The antiwar crowd characterized Vietnam military service as criminal, and this had devastating effects on domestic politics and the war effort. *The protests were demonizing and demoralizing our troops*.

Vietnamese monks immolated themselves in protest of the Diem regime. Jane Fonda and John Kerry spoke against the war. Communist-front groups publicly protested in the U.S. Radical activists, "Black pan-

Women, Hispanics, and Communists, in Vietnam antiwar protests.

thers," gays, labor, women-libbers, draft-age males, and civil rights groups supported the anti-war movement. Signs of the times!

Buddhist monk self immolation in Vietnam

Dr. Martin Luther King, Jr.

Seattle Black Panthers.

Vietnam Was A Just War

Veterans protest. The Civil Rights March in Wash. DC. 1963.

Joe Abodeely

National Guard at Kent State University, May 4, 1970.

Vietnam Was A Just War

1955[1]–The very first protests against U.S. involvement in Vietnam were in 1955, when United States Merchant Marine sailors condemned the U.S. government for the use of U.S. merchant ships to transport European troops to "subjugate the native population" of Vietnam.

1963–

- May. Anti-Vietnam War protests in England and Australia

- June 11. (Born Lâm Văn Túc) was a Vietnamese Mahayana Buddhist monk who burned himself to death at a busy Saigon road intersection. Quảng Đức was protesting the persecution of Buddhists by the South Vietnamese Christian government led by Ngô Đình Diệm.

- September 21. War Resisters League starts first U.S. protest against Vietnam. War and "anti-Buddhist terrorism" by the U.S.-supported South Vietnamese regime with a demonstration at the U.S. Mission to the UN in New York City.

- October 9. WRL and other groups turn out 300 pickets against a speech by Madame Ngo Dinh Nhu at the Waldorf-Astoria in New York City.

---
1. Wikipedia list. See credits for reference.

1964–

- March. A conference at Yale plans demonstrations on May 4.

- April 25. The *Internal Protector* published a pledge of draft resistance by some of the organizers.

- May 2. Hundreds of students demonstrated on New York's Times Square and from there went to the United Nations. Seven hundred marched in San Francisco. Smaller demonstrations took place in Boston, Madison, Wisconsin, and Seattle. These protests were organized by the Progressive Labor Party with help from the Young Socialist Alliance. The *May 2nd Movement* was the PLP's youth affiliate.

- May 12. Twelve young men in New York publicly burned their draft cards to protest the war—the first such act of war resistance.

- Fall. Free Speech Movement at the University of California at Berkley defended the right of students to carry out political organizing on campus. The founder: Mario Savio.

- Early August. White and black activists gathered

near Philadelphia, Mississippi, for the memorial service of three civil rights workers. Speakers bitterly spoke out against Johnson's use of force in Vietnam, comparing it to violence used against blacks in Mississippi.

- December 19. First coordinated nationwide protests against the Vietnam War included demonstrations in New York City sponsored by War Resisters League, Fellowship of Reconciliation, Committee for Nonviolent Action, the Socialist Party of America, and the Student Peace Union, and attended by 1500 people; San Francisco had 1000 people; Minneapolis, Miami, Austin, Sacramento, Philadelphia, Chicago, Washington, Boston, Cleveland, and other cities also had demonstrations..

1965–

- February 2–March. Protests at the University of Kansas, organized by the RA Student Peace Union.

- February 12–16. Anti-U.S. demonstrations in various cities in the world, "including a break-in at the U.S. embassy in Budapest, Hungary, by some 200 Asian and African students."

- March 15. A debate organized by the Inter-University Committee for a Public Hearing on Vietnam was held in Washington, D.C. Radio and television coverage.

- March 16. An 82-year-old Detroit woman named Alice Herz self-immolated to make a statement against the horrors of the war. She died ten days later.

- March 24. First SDS organized teach-in, at the University of Michigan at Ann Arbor. Three thousand students attended; the idea spread quickly.

- March. Berkeley, California: Jerry Rubin and Stephen Smale's Vietnam Day Committee (VDC) organized a huge protest of 35,000.

- April. Oklahoma college students sent out hundreds of thousands of pamphlets with pictures on them of dead babies in a combat zone to portray a message about battles taking place in Vietnam.

- April 17. The SDS-organized *March Against the Vietnam War* on Washington, D.C., was the largest anti-war demonstration in the U.S. to date with 15-20,000 people attending. Paul Potter demanded a radical change of society.

- May 5. Several hundred people carrying a black coffin marched to the Berkeley, California, draft board, and 40 men burned their draft cards.

- May 21–23. Vietnam Day Committee organized large teach-in at UC Berkeley. Ten to thirty thousand attended.

- May 22. The Berkeley draft board was visited again, with 19 men burning their cards. President Lyndon B. Johnson was hanged in effigy.

- Summer. Young blacks in McComb, Mississippi, learned one of their classmates was killed in Vietnam and distributed a leaflet saying, "No Mississippi Negroes should be fighting in Viet Nam for the White man's freedom."

- June. Richard Steinke, a West Point graduate in Vietnam, refused to board an aircraft taking him to a remote Vietnamese village, stating the war "is not worth a single American life."

- June 27. *End Your Silence*, an open letter in the *New York Times* by the group *Artists and Writers Protest Against the War in Vietnam*.

- July. The Vietnam Day Committee organized militant protest in Oakland, California, ended in an inglorious debacle when the organizers ended the march from Oakland to Berkeley to avoid a confrontation with police.

- July. A *Women Strike for Peace* delegation led by Cora Weiss met its North Vietnamese and Vietcong counterparts in Jakarta, Indonesia.

- July 30. A man from the Catholic Worker Movement was photographed burning his draft card on Whitehall Street in Manhattan in front of the Armed Forces Induction Center. His photograph appeared in *Life* magazine in August.

- October 15. David J. Miller burned his draft card at a rally held near the Armed Forces Induction Center on Whitehall Street in Manhattan. The 24-year-old pacifist, member of the Catholic Worker Movement, became the first man arrested and convicted under the 1965 amendment to the 1948 Selective Service Act.

- October 15–16. Europe, October 15–16. First *International Days of Protest*. Anti-U.S. demonstrations in London, Rome, Brussels, Copenhagen, and Stockholm.

- October 20. Stephen Lynn Smith, a student at

the University of Iowa, spoke to a rally at the Memorial Union in Iowa City, Iowa, and burned his draft card. He was arrested, found guilty, and put on three years of probation.

- October 30. Pro-Vietnam War march in New York City with 25,000.

- November 2. As thousands of employees were streaming out of the Pentagon building in Washington in the late afternoon, Norman Morrison, a thirty-two-year-old pacifist, father of three, stood below the third-floor windows of Secretary of Defense Robert McNamara, doused himself with kerosene, and set himself afire, giving up his life in protest against the war.

- November 6. Thomas C. Cornell, Marc Paul Edelman, Roy Lisker, David McReynolds, and James Wilson burned their draft cards at a public rally organized by the Committee for Non-Violent Action in Union Square, New York City.

- November 27. There was a SANE-sponsored *March on Washington* in 1965. There were 15-20,000 demonstrators.

- December 16–17. High school students in Des Moines, Iowa, were suspended for wearing black armbands to "mourn the deaths on both sides" and in support of Robert Kennedy's call for a Christmas truce. The students sued the Des Moines School District, resulting in the 1969 U.S. Supreme Court decision in favor of the students, *Tinker v. Des Moines*.

1966–From September 1965 to January 1970, 170,000 men were drafted and another 180,000 enlisted. By January, 2,000,000 men had secured college deferments.

- February. Local artists in Hollywood build a 60-foot tower of protest on Sunset Boulevard.

- March 25–26. Second *Days of International Protest*. Organized by the National Coordinating Committee to End the War in Vietnam, led by SANE, Women Strike for Peace, the Committee for Nonviolent Action and the SDS: 20,000 to 25,000 in New York alone, demonstrations also in Boston, Philadelphia, Washington, Chicago, Detroit, San Francisco, Oklahoma City. Abroad in Ottawa, London, Oslo, Stockholm, Lyon, and Tokyo.

- March 31. David Paul O'Brien and three companions burned their draft cards on the steps of the

South Boston Courthouse. The case was tried by the Supreme Court as *United States v. O'Brien*.

- Spring. Clergy and Laymen Concerned About Vietnam was founded.

- May 15. *March Against the Vietnam War*, led by SANE and Women Strike for Peace, with 8-10,000 taking part.

- Muhammad Ali (Cassius Clay) refused to go to war, famously stating that he had "no quarrel with the Viet Cong" and that "no Viet Cong ever called me nigger." Ali also stated he would not go "10,000 miles to help murder, kill, and burn other people to simply help continue the domination of white slave-masters over dark people." In 1967, he was sentenced to 5 years in prison but was released on appeal by the United States Supreme Court.

- Summer. Six members of the SNCC invade an induction center in Atlanta and were later arrested.

- July. First national anti-war *Mobilization Committee* was established.

- July 3. A crowd of over 4,000 demonstrated

outside of the U.S. Embassy in London. Scuffles broke out between the protesters and police, and at least 31 people were arrested.

- November 7. Protests against Robert McNamara at Harvard University.

- Late December. Student Mobilization Committee was formed.

1967–

- January 29–February 5. *Angry Arts Week*, by the Artists Protest group.

- March 25. Vietnam March. Dr. Benjamin Spock, Martin Luther King, Jr. led nearly 5,000 marchers through the Chicago Loop to protest U.S. policy in Vietnam. March 25, 1967.

- April 4. Martin Luther King, Jr., spoke at Riverside Church in New York about the war: "Beyond Vietnam: A Time to Break Silence." King stated that *"somehow this madness must cease. We must stop now. I speak as a child of God and brother to the suffering poor of Vietnam. I speak for those whose land is being laid waste, whose homes are being destroyed, whose culture is being subverted. I speak for the poor of America who are paying the double price of smashed hopes at home and death and corruption in Vietnam. I speak as a citizen of the world, for the world as it stands aghast at the path we have taken. I speak as an American to the leaders of my own nation. The great initiative in this war is ours. The initiative to stop it must be ours."*

- April 15. At Sheep Meadow, Central Park, New York City, about 60 young men including a few students from Cornell University came together to burn their draft cards in a Maxwell House coffee can. More joined them, including uniformed Green Beret Army Reservist, Gary Rader. As many as 158 cards were burned.

- April 15. *Spring Mobe* protested in New York City (300,000) and in San Francisco. Founded in November 1966 as the Spring Mobilization Committee to End the War in Vietnam. Its National director was Reverend James L. Bevel.

- May 20–21. Seven hundred activists at Spring Mobilization Conference, Washington, D.C. A National Mobilization Committee to End the War in Vietnam (the Mobe) was created.

- May and November. Sweden. *International War Crimes Tribunal*.

- June 1. The Vietnam Veterans Against the War formed. Veteran Jan Barry Crumb participated in a protest on April 7 called the *Fifth Avenue Peace Parade* in New York City. On May 30, Crumb and ten like-minded men attended a peace demonstration in Washington, D.C.

- June 23. *The Bond*, the first G.I. underground paper was established.

- June 23. Thirteen hundred police attacked 10,000 peace marchers at the Century Plaza Hotel in Los Angeles where President Lyndon B. Johnson was being honored.

- Summer of 1967. Neil Armstrong and various other NASA officials began a tour of South America to raise awareness for space travel. According to *First Man*, a biography of Armstrong's life, during the tour, several South American college students protested the astronaut, and shouted such phrases as "Murderers, get out of Vietnam!" and other anti-Vietnam War messages.

- October 16. A day of widespread war protest organized by The Mobe in 30 cities across the U.S. About 1,400 draft cards were burned.

- October 18. *Dow Day*, University of Wisconsin–Madison. This was the first university Vietnam War protest to turn violent. Thousands of students protested Dow Chemical (maker of napalm) recruiting on campus. Nineteen police officers and about 50 students were treated for injuries at hospitals.

- October 20. Resist leaders presented draft cards to the Department of Justice, Washington, D.C.

- October 21–23. National Mobe organized *The March on the Pentagon to Confront the War Makers*. One hundred thousand congregated at the Lincoln Memorial on the D.C. Mall; 35,000 (possibly up to 50,000) went on to the Pentagon, some to engage in acts of civil disobedience. Norman Mailer's *The Armies of the Night* described the event.

- October 27. Father Philip Berrigan, a Josephite priest and World War II veteran, led a group now known as the Baltimore Four who went to a draft board in Baltimore, Maryland, drenched the draft records with blood, and waited to be arrested.

- December 4. National draft card turn in. At San

Francisco's Federal Building, some 500 protesters witnessed 88 draft cards collected and burned.

- December 4–8. *Stop the Draft Week* demonstrations in New York. Five hundred and eighty-five arrested, amongst them Benjamin Spock.

- Sweden, December 20. Seventh Year of the Vietcong (the *Front National de Libération du Vietnam dU.S.ud*, or *FNL*) celebrated with violent clashes in Stockholm. Demonstrations in 40 Swedish towns.

1968–

- German students protested against the Vietnam War in 1968.

- Peace Corps volunteers in Chile spoke out against the war. Ninety-two volunteers defied the Peace Corps director and issued a circular denouncing the war.

- January. Singer Eartha Kitt, while at a luncheon at the White House, spoke out against the war and its effects on the youth, exclaiming, "you send the best of this country off to be shot and maimed," to her fellow guests. "They rebel in the street. They will take pot... and they will get high.

They don't want to go to school because they're going to be snatched off from their mothers to be shot in Vietnam."

- January 15. Jeannette Rankin led a demonstration of thousands of women in Washington, D.C.

- March 17. London, Sunday. There was a violent protest in London (street occupation), not supported by the Old Left. Over 300 arrests.

- April 2. Frankfurt, Germany, Gudrun Ensslin and Andreas Baader, joined by Thorwald Proll and Horst Sohnlein, set fire to two department stores.

- April 3. National draft card turn in. About 1,000 draft cards were turned in. In Boston, 15,000 protesters watched 235 men turn in their draft cards.

- April 4. Reverend Martin Luther King, Jr., assassinated.

- Late April. Student Mobe sponsored national student strike, demonstrations in New York and San Francisco.

- April–May. Occupation of five buildings at Columbia University. Future leading Weather

Underground member Mark Rudd gained prominence.

- April 11. Berlin, Germany. Rudi Dutschke was shot and wounded. Massive riots against Axel Springer publishers.

- May. FBI's COINTELPRO campaign was launched against the New Left.

- May. Agricultural Building at Southern Illinois University (SIU) was bombed.

- May 1. Boston University graduate Philip Supina wrote to his draft board in Tucson, Arizona, that he had "absolutely no intention to report for [his] exam, or for induction, or to aid in any way the American war effort against the people of Vietnam."

- May 17. Philip Berrigan and his brother, Daniel, led seven others into a draft board office in Catonsville, Maryland, removed records, and set them afire with homemade napalm outside in front of reporters and onlookers.

- June 4–5. Robert F. Kennedy, presidential candidate, who was the hope of the anti-war movement, was shot after winning the California primary. He died the next morning, June 6.

- Late June. Student Mobe ruptures.

- August 28. Democratic National Convention in Chicago. Violent clashes occurred.

- October 14, 1968. Presidio mutiny sit-down protest was carried out by 27 prisoners at the Presidio stockade in San Francisco, California.

- October 21. In Japan, a group of 290,000 activists occupied the ShinjukU.S.tation, protesting an earlier incident in August 1967 where a JNR freight train hauling kerosene to the Tachikawa Airbase collided with another train and exploded. The event, known as the ShinjukU.S.tation riots managed to disrupt all railway traffic at the station and led to clashes with riot police and acts of vandalism; it was the largest anti-war protest in Japan at the time.

- November 14. National draft card turn in.

1969–

- Major campus protests took place across the country during the whole year.

- January 19–20. Protests against Richard Nixon's inauguration.

- February 28. A group of Seattle Panthers led by Lt. Elmer Dixon gathered on the steps of the Capitol in Olympia to protest a bill that would make it a crime to exhibit firearms "in a manner manifesting an intent to intimidate others." In contrast to a California demonstration, they did not enter the building and they were not arrested.

- March 22. Nine protesters smashed glass, hurled files out a fourth floor window, and poured blood on files and furniture at the Dow Chemical offices in Washington, D.C.

- March 29. Conspiracy charges against eight suspected organizers of the Chicago Convention Protests.

- April 5–6. Anti-war demonstrations and parades in several cities, New York, San Francisco, Los Angeles, Washington, D.C. and others.

- May 21. Silver Spring Three–Les Bayless, John Bayless, and Michael Bransome walked into a Silver Spring, Maryland, Selective Service office where they destroyed several hundred draft records to protest the war.

- June. At Brown University commencement, two-thirds of the graduating class turned their backs when Henry Kissinger stood up to address them.

- June 8. The Old Main building at SIU burns to the ground. Units of firefighters from all over the area tried to salvage the building but could not put out the fire before everything was destroyed.

- June. Chicago. SDS national convention. The SDS disintegrates into SDS-WSA and SDS. The Worker Student Alliance of the Progressive Labor Party (PLP) has the majority of delegates (900) on its side. The smaller Revolutionary Youth Movement faction (500) divides into RYM-I/Weatherman, who retained control of the SDS National Office, and Maoist RYM-II. This faction will further divide into the various groups of New Communist Movement. There were several anti-war organizations.

- July 4–5. Cleveland. The national anti-war conference established the National Mobilization Committee to End the War in Vietnam.

- October 8–11. Weatherman's disastrous *Days of Rage* in Chicago. Only 300 militants show up, not the expected 10,000. 287 were arrested.

- October 15. *National Moratorium Against the War demonstrations*. Huge crowds in Washington and in Boston (100,000). Anti-war Senator, George McGovern, spoke to a large crowd in Boston.

- November 15. The *Mobe's Moratorium to End the War in Vietnam* mobilizes 500,000. *March Against Death*, Washington, D.C.

- November 15. San Francisco march.

- November 26. Draft-lottery bill signed.

- December 1. The U.S. Selective Service System conducted two lotteries.

- December 7. The 5th Dimension performs their song *Declaration* on the *Ed Sullivan Show*. The opening of the Declaration of Independence (for their future security) said that it was a right and duty to revolt against despotism.

1970–

- February, March. Wave of bombings across the USA.

- March. Anti-draft protests across the USA.

- March 14. Two American merchant marine sailors named Clyde McKay and Alvin Glatkowski seized the *SS Columbia Eagle* and forced the master to sail to Cambodia as opposed to Thailand, where it was on its way to deliver napalm bombs for the U.S. Air Force in Vietnam.

- April. New Mobe Moratorium and SMC protests across the country.

- April 4. A right-wing *Victory March*, organized by Reverend Carl McIntire calls for victory in the Vietnam War. 50,000 attend.

- April 19. Moratorium announces disbanding.

- May 2. Violent anti-war rallies at many universities.

- May 4. Kent State University, Ohio. Kent State Shootings—U.S. National Guard killed four young people during a demonstration. As a result, four million students went on strike at more than 450 universities and colleges. The best-known cultural response to the deaths at Kent State was the protest song *Ohio*, written by Neil Young for Crosby, Stills, Nash & Young.

- May 8. New York. *Hard Hat Riot*: after a student anti-war demonstration, workers attacked them and rioted for two hours.

- May 9. Mobe sponsored *Kent State/Cambodia Incursion Protest*, Washington, D.C. Seventy-five to 100,000 demonstrators converged on Washington, D.C., to protest the Kent State shootings and the Nixon administration's incursion into Cambodia. Even though the demonstration was quickly put together, protesters were still able to bring out thousands to march in the Capital. It was an almost spontaneous response to the events of the previous week. Police ringed the White House with buses to block the demonstrators from getting too close to the executive mansion. Early in the morning before the march, Nixon met with protesters briefly at the Lincoln Memorial.

- May 14. Jackson State College. Jackson State killings: Two dead and twelve injured during violent protests.

- May 20. New York. An estimated 60,000 to 150,000 went at a pro-war demonstration on Wall Street.

- May 28. University of Tennessee, Knoxville, TN. Nixon at Billy Graham Crusade in Neyland Stadium where 800 Students carried "ThoU.S.halt Not Kill" signs into the stadium. Many are arrested and charged with "disrupting a religious service" with only Republican candidates on the stage with Graham and Nixon.

- June. At commencement for the University of Massachusetts, students stenciled red fists of protests, white peace symbols, and blue doves onto their black gowns.

- August 24. University of Wisconsin–Madison. Sterling Hall bombing: aimed at the Army Math Research Center on the second, third, and fourth floors of the building. In missing its target, a Ford van packed with explosives hit the physics laboratory on the first floor and killed young researcher, Robert Fassnacht, and seriously injured another person.

- August 29. *Chicano Moratorium*. Twenty to thirty thousand Mexican-Americans participated in the largest anti-war demonstration in Los Angeles. Police are attacked with clubs and guns and kill three people, including Rubén Salazar, a TV news director and *LA Times* reporter.

1971–

- March 1. Weatherman planted a bomb in the Capitol building in Washington, D.C., causing $300,000 in damage, but no casualties.

- April. The Vancouver Indo-Chinese Women's Conference (VICWC), a six-day protest, gathered close to a thousand women.

- April 19–23. Vietnam Veterans Against the War (VVAW) staged operation *Dewey Canyon III*. A thousand camped on the National Mall.

- April 22–28. VVAW (and John Kerry) testified before Congress.

- April 24. *Peaceful Vietnam War Out Now* rally in Washington, D.C., on National Mall with 200,000 calling for an end to the Vietnam War. On the West Coast, in San Francisco, 156,000 participate in the largest demonstration so far.

- April 26. More militant attempts in Washington, D. C., to shut down the government were futile against 5,000 police and 12,000 troops.

- April 30. Anti-war protesters at the Justice Department.

- May. The Vietnam War was the longest military engagement Australia had ever participated in and many ordinary Australians were opposed to it. The demonstration in Melbourne, led by Member for Parliament Jim Cairns, saw over 100,000 people take to the streets for a peaceful occupation of the city. Across Australia, it was estimated that 200,000 people took part.

- May 3–5. *May Day Protests.* Planned by Rennie Davis and Jerry Coffin of the War Resisters League, later joined by Michael Lerner; militant mass action tried to shut down the government in Washington, D.C. Twelve thousand six hundred fourteen were arrested, a record in American history.

- August. A group of nuns, priests, and laypeople raided a draft board in Camden, New Jersey. They came to be known as the Camden 28.

- November 6. Toronto, Canada.

1972–

- April 15–20. May. New waves of protests across the country. Eight hundred National Guardsmen were ordered onto campus.

- May 11. Frankfurt am Main, Germany, Headquarters of the V Corps at the IG Farben Building. The *Commando Petra Schelm* of the *Rote Armee Fraktion* killed U.S. Officer Paul Bloomquist and wounded thirteen in a bombing attack.

- May 21. *Emergency March* on Washington, D.C., organized by the National Peace Action Coalition and the People's Coalition for Peace and Justice. Eight to fifteen thousand protested in Washington, D.C., against increased bombing of North Vietnam and the mining of its harbors.

- May 24. Heidelberg, Germany. The Red Army Faction detonated two car bombs at the European Headquarters of the US Army, killing three.

- June 22. *Ring Around Congress* demonstration, Washington, D.C.

- In July. Jane Fonda visited North Vietnam and spoke on Hanoi Radio, earning herself the nickname "Hanoi Jane."

- August 22. Three thousand protested against the 1972 Republican National Convention in Miami Beach. Ron Kovic, a wheelchair-bound Vietnam veteran, led fellow veterans into the Convention

Hall, wheeled down the aisles, and as Nixon began his acceptance speech shouted, "Stop the bombing! Stop the war!"

- October 14. The *Peace March to End the Vietnam War* was held in San Francisco. This demonstration began at City Hall and moved down Fulton Street to Golden Gate Park, where speeches were given. Over 2,000 were in attendance. Numerous groups (including veterans) marched to support the so-called "7-Point" plan to peace. George McGovern had given a speech at the Cow Palace the night before, which energized the Saturday morning event.

- November 7. General Election day. President Nixon beat George McGovern in a landslide election victory, with 60.7% popular votes and 520 electoral votes.

- December. There were protests against Hanoi and Haiphong bombings.

1973–

- January 20. Second inauguration of Richard Nixon. Inauguration protests, *March Against Racism & the War* in Washington, D.C.

Orthodox Versus Revisionist Views on Vietnam

Academic curricula during the 1960s and 1970s skewed the image of the war, and this was the primary cause of misinformation about the Vietnam War by so-called scholars.

Antiwar history faculty were called "Orthodox" historians who made biased presentations of the war in schools and in the media. Vietnam veterans or war supporters did not get jobs in academia or journalism to present a balanced presentation of the Vietnam War.

"Orthodox" historians claimed the war caused long-term psychological damage on many U.S. Veterans and depicted President Diem's government as illegitimate, the war to be reprehensible, and draft dodging sensible. Escaping service in the Vietnam War, most antiwar protesters were college students from middle or upper-class families and did not distinguish between the war and its combatants. Military Deferments or postponements to avoid Vietnam service favored the wealthy and well-educated who regarded U.S. soldiers as ready and willing killers or ignorant dupes.

Veterans' organizations and prospective employers initially shunned Vietnam veterans as did academia, who claimed diversity and thought "reasonable" people shared their antiwar view.

Vietnam veterans were often students who had to work their way through college on a part-time basis, and they could not get deferments.

Most of them in the 1960s and early 1970s came from a poor or working-class background and had only a high school education, but they were the most educated veterans in U.S. history. ***Two-thirds of Vietnam veterans volunteered, and more than half returned to school after their service in Vietnam.***

The orthodox (antiwar) view is still taught in schools, while movies and television ignore or often portray Vietnam veterans' service negatively. Ken Burns' propaganda film, *Vietnam*, has Communist operatives and antiwar types stating their views, but very few pro-U.S. views were presented. The film disparaged the Vietnam War and Vietnam veterans and lauded the anti-war protesters.

In the fall of 1963, the antiwar crowd publicly disparaged President Diem and his government claiming that the Republic of Viet Nam would be better off without him. Afterward, the media piled on.

The uncritical acceptance of the dubious and deceptive writings of David Halberstam, Neil Sheehan, and Stanley Karnow who reported on the war as it happened and whose so-called history was destructive to U.S. efforts in Vietnam is still a problem today. They were journalists, not historians, who later wrote best-selling books. Halberstam, Sheehan, Karnow, and other so-called "orthodox" authors, wrote about the era from Vietnam's division into north and south in 1954 to Tet in 1968, and they gave minimal coverage of 1969 to 1975, probably due to U.S. and ARVN troops success against the VC and NVA.

Halberstam printed negative material before the other journalists did—*The Making of a Quagmire* in 1964, *Ho*, in 1971, and *The Best and the Brightest*, in 1972. Karnow published *Vietnam: a History*, a multi-volume PBS documentary in 1983, selling over one million copies. Sheehan's, *A Bright Shining Lie*, in 1988, won the national book award and Pulitzer prize. These journalists thought Diem was not liberal enough in dealing with the press and Buddhist protesters. They didn't believe Diem's claim that the Communists infiltrated the Buddhists, but the Communists later admitted that they did. In November 1963, Buddhist generals got JFK's approval to kill Diem in a coup—three weeks before JFK's assassination.

ARVNs defeated the fourteen North Vietnamese divisions offensive in the spring of 1972 until being ordered to withdraw and defend Saigon before the Peace accords. Most people don't know this.

Historians opposing the orthodox view and justifying U.S. Vietnam service were called revisionist "propagandists" or *"Revisionists"* by the orthodox crowd. The Revisionists were a small group of academic historians and veterans who rejected the basic tenets of the antiwar movement. In the late 1990s, they produced works and histories showing South Vietnam making progress and getting stronger by the early 1970s and wiping out the VC.

Documentation grew, revisionist scholarship improved, more truth about the war emerged, and revisionist numbers increased; but the movement did not make inroads into academia. Recent revisionist histories were well-documented, but some college faculties failed to give them consideration.

The following are some "revisionists" of note.

Dr. Mark Moyar, former director—USAID office of civilian-military cooperation—authored several books and worked extensively on national security affairs, international development, foreign aid, and capacity building. His article, "Vietnam: Historians at War," about journalists misrepresenting the Vietnam War, is elucidating. The following are other example of "revisionists."

Marguerite Higgins, the first female war correspondent to win the Pulitzer Prize reporting on the Korean War, saw that Halberstam's articles had clear mistakes tarnishing President Diem. She authored *New York Herald Tribune* stories exposing Halberstam.

The *Times* editor sent Halberstam a letter saying Higgins' writing balanced the negative material from Saigon. He wanted Halberstam to respond, and an infuriated Halberstam threatened to quit if they published Higgins' articles. Higgins wrote a book in 1965 entitled *Our Vietnam Nightmare*; it faded into obscurity.

A small group of revisionist books emerged in the 1970s and 1980s. Many of their authors had doctorates, but few had permanent academic appointments.

Robert F. Turner, a Vietnam veteran, Hoover Institution fellow, worked in Britain in a history department less politicized than in the U.S. He later got a non-tenured position at the University of Virginia Law

School and disputed that the Vietnamese Communists were devoted nationalists in his book *Vietnamese Communism: Its Origins and Development.*

Ralph Smith, distinguished British professor, whose international history of the war, argued that Vietnamese Communism was a serious threat to the U.S. and **Norman Podhoretz**, the American pundit, were other "revisionist" writers who made the same argument in a more academically focused work.

Ellen Hammer and William Colby, an American scholar living in France and a former CIA director, respectively, alleged South Vietnam was viable under Diem and the U.S. seriously erred in inspiring his demise.

Harry Summers, a retired U.S. Army Colonel, and former President Nixon argued the war could have been won had the U.S. taken more aggressive military actions to sever the Ho Chi Minh trail in Laos and increase massive bombing in North Vietnam. History has shown that they were right.

Guenter Lewy's *America and Vietnam*, the most influential of the early revisionist books, was the refutation of antiwar arguments about the immorality, inhumanity, and illegality of U.S. military actions in Vietnam. After Lewy's book, countless trendy anti-war arguments stopped appearing in the articles and books written by the antiwar authors.

Arthur Dommen's *The Indochinese Experience of the French and the Americans: Nationalism and Communism in Cambodia, Laos, and Vietnam* is the longest work of recent revisionism. A journalist in RVN and Laos during the war, he later obtained a Ph.D. in agricultural economics, and spent years gathering information. He debunked the Halberstam-Sheehan-Karnow accounts, stressed the evils of Communism, and decided Diem, a nationalist, and his supporters, was a viable leader. He spoke about Buddhist protesters making up evidence of religious oppression and stifling religious freedom to hurt Diem's government from 1963 to 1965.

Lewis Sorley, a U.S. Army and CIA veteran with a Ph.D., but no academic affiliation, wrote about regular and irregular elements of the war during its latter years in, *A Better War*. He supported revisionists' views that Vietnam could have survived if the U.S. had not cut aid to it in the war's final years because, as the U.S. withdrew, ARVN forces defeated a massive offensive by fourteen NVA divisions in the spring of 1972—an event orthodox historians ignored.

B.G. Burkett, a Vietnam veteran and a stockbroker by profession, demolished much mythology about

Vietnam veterans in, *Stolen Valor*, a book based on detailed research which showed that several hundred supposed Vietnam veterans in the public spotlight were frauds. He used statistics to disprove orthodox historians' generalizations that Vietnam veterans had much higher rates of unemployment, homelessness, and suicide than non-veterans.

Journalists, academicians, and media propagandized the U.S. war effort in Vietnam branding it as illegal because it was not a Congressionally "declared" war, but consider that Congress did not declare the following wars:

- Harry S. Truman (in office 1950-1953) Korean War

- Dwight D. Eisenhower-(in office 1953-1961) Cold War

- John F. Kennedy (in office 1961-1963) Bay of Pigs incident

- Lyndon Baynes Johnson (in office 1963-1969) escalated the Vietnam War

- Richard M. Nixon (in office 1969-1974) "War on Drugs" (1971) withdrew troops from Vietnam

- Ronald Reagan (in office 1981-1989) sent troops to Grenada, Central America, Lebanon, Libya

- George H. W. Bush (in office 1989-1993) Persian Gulf War I with Iraq (1990)

- Bill Clinton (in office 1993-2001) Persian Gulf War II in Iraq (1999); Bosnian War; Kosovo

- George W. Bush (in office 2001-2009) War on Terror; Afghanistan (Taliban and Al Qaeda); Iraq

- Barrack Obama (in office 2009-2017) Syria; Libya Civil War (2011), Operations Odyssey Dawn; Unified Protector.

The Vietnam War Isn't Over

I had a college education before I was a soldier in the war and understood the geopolitics of the times. In the 1960s, since a war was coming, I enrolled in ROTC, graduated from college in 1965 as a 2nd Lieutenant, Infantry, did some studies in law and graduate school, and arrived in Vietnam in January 1968. I served with the 1st Air Cavalry Division as a combat infantry unit commander.

When I returned home from Vietnam in January 1969, the antiwar movement was in full momentum. I was in the University of Arizona Law School and spoke up for Vietnam veterans at a rally at school during the "moratorium" activities. I was mocked, booed, and shouted down for being a "Vietnam vet" in "an illegal war" risking my life for my country. How could I be maligned for doing my patriotic duty?

Once, when I went to the Student Union, two Jewish law students, who knew I served in Vietnam, were sitting at a nearby table. They talked loudly to ensure that I could hear, and they proclaimed how they would *fight for Israel but not serve in Vietnam.* I was shocked by this loyalty to another country over America; but I knew they were mocking me.

Many years later, after I graduated from law school and practiced law for decades in Phoenix, I designed a four-panel history of the Vietnam War Memorial for the Arizona State Capitol Memorial Park. At a hearing regarding its construction, two women on the State Memorial Commission objected to its placement, but it was finally approved, and it is in place on the mall. An organization sponsored historical talks by approved speakers, and I applied several times to give talks on Vietnam as I had done numerous times over the years. I never even got a reply.

In 2012, the Arizona Department of Veterans Services and I started dinners honoring Vietnam veterans as part of the 50th Commemoration of the Vietnam War. The ADVS Director, a Vietnam veteran, supported and funded the project, but he was replaced by a new female director who had been an Air Force Reservist, and she did not support our program. She cut our funding. I got funding elsewhere to continue the program. I have experienced *gender bias against males and Vietnam veterans* in other contexts, too.

Our military museum displayed Vietnam artifacts

and replica weapons at a convention center for the Museums Association of America. Some women complained about our Vietnam display *simply for relating to Vietnam*. Fortunately, the convention center ignored their complaints, but there still was an irrational prejudice against the Vietnam War in the community. I have refused to support MAA ever since.

When the legislature confirmed the governor's appointees to serve on the state historical society board, a female candidate to the board disparaged my Vietnam service to me in private on the day we were confirmed. She became Treasurer on the board.

In another instance, I offered to write an article on Vietnam for the Arizona Historical Society journal since I have authored several published pieces on the war. The editor rejected it, but he allowed a Vietnam display in the history museum in Tucson. As a Tucson native, I was grateful for his decision. A few weeks later, I was modifying that Vietnam display at AHS when a docent approached me and said the display should not even be in the museum. He maligned the war and those who served in it. I politely defended the display and then ignored him. The display remained for several weeks.

The president of the AHS board gave his opinion that my name should not have been in the Vietnam display, but the uniform and news articles had my name, and I am a Tucson native. It was all history. It was what it was.

Another time, I was invited to be a guest speaker for Veterans Day at a retirement community in Chandler, Arizona. I gave a power-point presentation on the Vietnam War, left it with the hosts, and later got an email from the female host saying she wanted to do a less "political" program. This was "code" for "not to do a presentation relating to Vietnam."

All wars are "political"—the Vietnam War was no different than other wars—WW I, WW II, Korea, and all the Middle East wars—because Vietnam was as much a "just war" as any of them, but an entire generation of patriots was denigrated and still is.

I have a Juris Doctor, practiced law for half a century, written two award-winning books on Vietnam, written several articles or contributed to them about Vietnam, and started the Arizona Military Museum in 1980 with Vietnam as its first display. I am a 79-year-old Vietnam veteran. I am proud to have served my country in the Vietnam War, and I am proud of the others who did, too. We honor veterans of other wars, but the Vietnam War and those who served in it are almost totally forgotten. I've done about all I can do to honor those who served "across the pond". Apparently, it has not been good enough.

Pundits, media personalities, and many so-called "historians" opine that "America lost" the Vietnam War thereby showing their ignorance of war and geopolitics. As previously noted, ***"Vietnam" was two wars—one in Vietnam and one in America.***

The American military and President Nixon secured "peace with honor" in Vietnam, but political factions in the U.S. were satisfied with undermining the successes of U.S. military personnel to defame Nixon. They were also unsympathetic and complacent about disparaging and discarding the service of young Americans who risked their lives, won the battles, and achieved peace before they returned home.

Those who honorably served in combat risking life, limb, and fortune in Vietnam or in any other legitimate military action should be treated with respect, not scorn. This should be a major lesson learned from the Vietnam experience. Be aware of the "fakers," trouble-makers, and wannabes, and if you must, damn the war, not the warrior!

Appendix

Appendix 1

Arizona Vietnam Veterans Memorial

The dedication of the Vietnam Memorial on March 29, 2016 adds to, updates, and completes the Arizona Vietnam Memorial site. The first phase (1980s) was a tribute to the fallen Arizona veterans with their names memorialized on granite walls and the statues of the three soldiers. The second phase (1990s) was a series of bronze plaques showing the timeline of key events in the war.

The third phase (March 29, 2016) was dedicated on Arizona Vietnam Veterans' Day. This third phase honors all Vietnam veterans by explaining the geopolitics, media influence, results of the antiwar movement, and the extraordinary service of Vietnam veterans under the circumstances of the times. *It gives meaning to Vietnam veterans' service to help heal a "wounded spirit" by educating the public and future veterans*.

Joe Abodeely

Arizona Vietnam Veterans Memorial
Wesley Bolin Memorial Park Phoenix, Arizona

Vietnam Was A Just War

The following text is on the four stainless steel plaques on the memorial.

Honoring Vietnam Veterans

The plight of the South Vietnamese people and the valiant service of their military who fought for the duration of the war has never been fully considered or appreciated by the vast majority of the American public.

The word "Vietnam" has many connotations—the history, the country, the era, the war, the politics—and it is a complex and emotional subject for many to address, and there are many perspectives.

So, how did the Vietnam War become America's only "bad war?" The reason should not be because America "lost the war" since the military won the war in 1973. It has been said, "The first casualty of war is truth."

Some Key Historical and Geopolitical Facts

France had colonized Vietnam since the mid-1800s, and after WWII, the U.S. and France wanted to prevent Communist takeover of Vietnam. On March 6, 1946, France recognized Vietnam as a free state, but not an independent state, and agreed with a Leninist front to enter into negotiations on the future status of Indochina. The Leninist front wanted to unite all of Vietnam under Communist rule although the Vietnamese had never been a "united" people. By December 1946, the French Indo-Chinese War had begun.

On June 5, 1948, France agreed to recognize an independent "State of Vietnam" within the French Union with former Emperor Bao Dai as its head, and on February 7, 1950, the United States recognized this "State of Vietnam" as an independent state within the French Union. During the same year, the Soviet Union recognized the Vietminh regime in North Vietnam as The Democratic Republic of Vietnam. Each regime claimed authority over the whole of Vietnam. In 1954, the French Indo-Chinese War ended in military defeat for the French Union Forces at Dien Bien Phu and in political capitulation at the Geneva Conference. The 1954 Geneva Accords drew a demilitarized zone and required phased regroupment of Vietminh Forces from the south to the north. But the Vietminh remained in the south later forming, under instructions from Hanoi, the National Liberation Front (NLF).

Also, in 1954, the U.S. and several other nations signed the SEATO Treaty which obligated the U.S. to defend South Vietnam against Communist aggression. A treaty is "the supreme law of the land" and was one of the major reasons why the U.S. military acted in its national interest without a declaration of war by Congress.

On Dec. 20, 1960, The National Liberation Front (NLF)—a Communist Vietnamese political organization—was formed to effect the overthrow of the South Vietnamese government.

In January 1961, newly elected President John F. Kennedy pledged to the world:

"Let every nation know, whether it wishes us well or ill, that we shall pay any price, bear any burden, meet any hardship, support any friend, oppose any foe, to assure the survival and the success of liberty."

In 1962, Hanoi published the Third Party Congress' multi-volume proceedings in English and mailed copies to many American university libraries. Volume I noted that the Communist Party passed a resolution for "our people" in the south to set up a "national united front" in South Vietnam under the leadership of a Marxist-Leninist party.

Some alleged that LBJ either fabricated or provoked the so-called "attack" in the Gulf of Tonkin on the *U.S.S. Maddox* on August 2, 1964—but after the war, North Vietnamese Defense Minister Vo Nguyen Giap told Robert McNamara that the attack occurred.

In August 1964, Congress enacted the Southeast Asian Resolution by a vote of 504-2 because of the Gulf of Tonkin incident which involved attacks on two U.S. destroyers. Congress' joint resolution made clear the United States was responding to *"a deliberate and systematic campaign of aggression"* by Hanoi, and this attack was another reason for the U.S. involvement in Vietnam.

The 1965 State Department's February "white paper" titled "Aggression from the North" was called a "lie" by scholars who portrayed the conflict as a struggle within South Vietnam for "freedom" and "human rights."

A 1967 Hanoi English-language translation of the NLF Program matched paragraphs verbatim with Hanoi's English translation of the 1955 Fatherland Front program. The NLF flag was a direct copy of Hanoi's flag except for adding some blue to the background. Hanoi wanted Communist domination over South Vietnam.

There were several years of bitter fighting in

Vietnam in which the average infantryman served 240 days under hostile fire in only one year while an average infantryman in WWII served only 40 days in combat in four years. The point is to emphasize that Vietnam veterans' service was extraordinary.

Eventually, due to extensive U.S. bombing of Hanoi and Haiphong Harbor, the U.S. and its allies forced North Vietnam to sign the Paris Peace Accords in January, 1973.

South Vietnam got some concessions, the U.S. got its POWs back, and the U.S. promised to continue to resupply South Vietnam with weapons, ammunition, and equipment if North Vietnam renewed its aggression. The vast majority of U.S forces left Vietnam in 1973, having won its involvement in the war then.

In May 1973, Congress ceased all logistical support to South Vietnam preventing it from defending itself. Our Vietnamese allies fought valiantly as long as they could until they ran out of ammunition and supplies. North Vietnam took over South Vietnam two years later on April 30, 1975.

Joe Abodeely

Media "Spin" Influenced the Public and the War

Vietnam was the first televised war to "inform" the public as it reported the brutality of the war every night on the evening news. The post WWII baby-boomers' idealism was shattered by images and horror of war brought into their homes as they saw the blood and napalm while eating dinner. Some draft-eligible men ran off to Canada or took other actions not to get drafted.

A cultural revolution in the U.S. was also going on at the same time involving civil rights, women's liberation, and farm-workers' rights, which all complemented the anti-war fervor of the times. The media, the anti-war protestors, and the counter-culture-types fed off of each other as they maligned the Vietnam War and its servicemen, and very few anti-Vietnam War protesters had any idea they were echoing Hanoi's propaganda lines and were Communist dupes—NOT heroes.

Ho Chi Minh

The media presented Ho Chi Minh as a hero—a "freedom fighter" and the George Washington of his country—but he actually was an ardent Communist who spent two decades as a paid agent of the Communist International traveling around the globe doing

Moscow's bidding. Nationalist Vietnamese patriots who resisted Ho's demands were often either murdered or—prior to the French withdrawal in 1954—betrayed to French colonial authorities for French francs.

Walter Cronkite and the Tet Offensive

The Tet Offensive of 1968 was a series of attacks by Viet Cong and North Vietnamese Army forces at various locations in South Vietnam to incite a mass uprising against the South Vietnamese government. The offensive failed miserably as U.S. forces and Vietnamese allies actually won, but Walter Cronkite erroneously reported that the enemy won the 1968 Tet Offensive:

> *"Who won and who lost in the great Tet Offensive against the cities? I'm not sure. The Vietcong did not win by a knockout, but neither did we. The referees of history may make it a draw. It seems now more certain than ever that the bloody experience of Vietnam is to end in a stalemate. But it is increasingly clear to this reporter that the only rational way out then will be to negotiate, not as victors, but as honorable people who lived up to their pledge to defend democracy and did the best they could."*

Cronkite simply misstated the result of the battle. Not all Americans were against the war, but the Tet Offensive of 1968 and the Battle of Hue were the turning point, and Walter Cronkite, the most trusted man in America, through the power of television, enhanced the negative perception of the war.

During the months and years that followed the Battle of Hue, which began on January 31, 1968, and lasted a total of 26 days, dozens of mass graves were discovered in and around Hue. The death toll of the victims was estimated between 2,800 to 6,000 civilians and prisoners of war and included women, men, children, and infants. The Republic of Vietnam released a list of 4,062 victims identified as having been either murdered or abducted. Victims were found bound, tortured, clubbed to death, and sometimes buried alive. The media did not emphasize the Hue massacre as much as they did My Lai.

My Lai

The My Lai incident involved an American infantry unit gathering civilians and executing them in March 1968. The unit had suffered severe casualties in the area, and this was "payback." It was a horrendous war crime and was presented as typical of Vietnam soldiers' service when it was not routine for infantry units to do mass executions of civilians.

The death, destruction, and the killing of innocent civilians in the Vietnam War should not be an iconic image and legacy of Vietnam veterans' service any more than the killing of innocent civilians which occurred in Dresden, Tokyo, Hiroshima, Nagasaki, or Iraq during "Shock and Awe" should be. Innocent people are killed in all wars. We now call it "collateral damage." The My Lai incident became a rallying cry for the protestors, and television strongly influenced the results of the Vietnam War.

The Pentagon Papers

The *Pentagon Papers* were published in 1971 when support for the U.S. role in the war was steadily eroding, supposedly confirming that the U.S. government had instigated the conflict. Daniel Ellsberg, a U.S. Marine Corps officer from 1954 to 1957, worked as a strategic analyst at the RAND Corporation and the Department of Defense. He was an early supporter of U.S. involvement in Indochina, and he worked on the preparation of the 1967 classified study—the *Pentagon Papers*—of the United States' political and military involvement in Vietnam from the end of World War II.

By 1969, Ellsberg concluded the war in Vietnam was unwinnable and he secretly photocopied portions of the report and gave them to *The New York Times*. Beginning on June 13, 1971, the *Times* published a series of daily articles based on the *Pentagon Papers* as did the *Washington Post, Boston Globe*, and other newspapers, and the *Pentagon Papers* were read aloud in the public record in a Senate subcommittee hearing.

The *Pentagon Papers* showed that former Presidents had not fully disclosed to the public about the degree of U.S. involvement in Vietnam, from Truman's decision to give military aid to France fighting the communist-led Viet Minh to Johnson's development of plans to escalate the war in Vietnam as early as 1964. This confirmed many people's suspicions about the active role the U.S. government had taken in building up the conflict. (Remember that the NLF was formed on Dec. 20, 1960, four years earlier).

Ellsberg was indicted on criminal charges including conspiracy, espionage, and stealing government property. The trial began in 1973 but ended in a dismissal of the charges after prosecutors discovered that a secret White House team (dubbed "the plumbers") had burglarized Ellsberg's psychiatrist's office in September 1971 to find information to discredit him. The failure to disclose military secrets was "much ado about nothing," but it aided the anti-war movement.

General Loan Executing the Vietcong Officer

During the war, the media published photos without explanation which supported the anti-war movement. The famous photo of National Police Chief Brig. Gen. Nguyen Ngoc Loan executing the Vietcong officer on February 1, 1968 was taken by Eddie Adams who later said that General Loan *"shot him in the head and walked away. And walked by us and said, 'They killed many of my men and many of our people.'"*

The Viet Cong lieutenant had just beheaded a South Vietnamese colonel and killed his wife and their six children. Adams' photograph became a symbol of the excesses of the war. But for the rest of his life, Adams was haunted by the photo and felt it was misunderstood. Adams said: *"If you're this man, this general, and you just caught this guy after he killed some of your people… How do you know you wouldn't have pulled that trigger yourself? You have to put yourself in that situation… It's a war."*

Joe Abodeely

The "Napalm Girl"

The "napalm girl," Kim Phuc, was the naked girl running from an airborne attack in the devastatingly iconic Pulitzer Prize-winning photo shot during the Vietnam War. It was June 8, 1972, when Phuc heard the soldier's scream: "We have to run out of this place! They will bomb here, and we will be dead!" Seconds later, she saw the tails of yellow and purple smoke grenades curling around the Cao Dai where her family had sheltered for three days as North and South Vietnamese forces fought for control of their village.

Part of the propaganda was that the U.S. Air Force dropped the bombs. The truth is the South Vietnamese Air Force conducted the mission because South Vietnamese troops called for an airstrike on that location to kill the North Vietnamese who were there. The "napalm girl" was an unintended casualty of war.

General William C. Westmoreland Versus CBS

CBS aired the program—*The Uncounted Enemy: A Vietnam Deception*—on January 23, 1982 to prove that General William C. Westmoreland deliberately misled President Johnson, the Pentagon, and Americans as to the actual strength of the VC/NVA just prior to the

1968 Tet Offensive to give the false impression that the U.S. was winning the war. It was the first big smear of a public figure attempted by CBS, but the U.S. and South Vietnam actually won the 1968 Tet Offensive.

George Crile produced and Mike Wallace narrated the program based on allegations by former CIA analyst and well-known left-winger, Sam Adams, whose claims had already been investigated and dismissed by the House Select Committee on Intelligence in 1975. CBS proceeded with production knowingly using a discredited source. It featured paid, coached, and rehearsed "witnesses" and Dan Rather deliberately provoking General Westmoreland to make him angry and appear "guilty" under his questioning.

After its controversial airing, *TV Guide* ran a major article titled "Anatomy of a Smear: How CBS Broke the Rules and 'Got' Westmoreland." Professor Leonard Magruder, then teaching at Suffolk College, wrote a detailed analysis of the lies. He sent copies to CBS executives, reporters, other networks, and major newspapers.

General Westmoreland received a copy of Professor Magruder's work and sent it to his lawyers, who were working on a $120 million libel suit against CBS. The general had tremendous support from fellow Vietnam veterans and Americans who raised thousands of dollars for his defense fund. General Westmoreland made a public statement on December 27, 1983 listing some of the exhibits in his lawsuit which were extremely damning to CBS, but because the cost of a lawsuit was prohibitive, he settled for an apology from CBS, much to the frustration of his many supporters.

He was magnanimous saying that "I do not believe it is fair to judge the media by the isolated actions of some of its irresponsible members." This major media attempt at smearing General Westmoreland failed miserably and showed despicable media conduct even after the war.

The Legacy of the So-called "Peace Movement"

In May 1973, right after the U.S. got North Vietnam to sign a peace treaty, Congress gave in to pressures from the "peace movement" and made it unlawful to spend appropriated funds on combat operations on the ground, in the air, or off the shores of North Vietnam, South Vietnam, Laos, or Cambodia. By doing so, Congress forfeited U.S. victory that the military won and betrayed the people whom six U.S. Presidents had repeatedly pledged their honor to protect.

Vietnam Was A Just War

Although the South Vietnamese still had planes, tanks, and rifles, they had very little fuel, spare parts, or ammo. They ran out of ammo in battle. The Communists launched a conventional military invasion behind columns of Soviet-made tanks to conquer South Vietnam in 1975. The media portrayed Vietnam veterans as having lost the Vietnam War.

So, what was the "human cost? The Communists took Laos and Cambodia at the same time. There was also Communist aggression in Angola, Central America, and Afghanistan—all direct consequences of the perception that America had lost its will during "Vietnam." These conflicts cost more than a million additional people's lives.

The Yale University Cambodia Genocide Project stated about 1.7 million Cambodians (more than 20% of the population) were killed by the "Red Cambodians" (Khmer Rouge) under Pol Pot. A *National Geographic Today* 2004 story captured the reality of the "killing fields" of Cambodia noting that, to save bullets, small children were simply picked up by their legs and bashed against trees until they stopped quivering. This was another consequence of the American "peace movement."

In "liberated" South Vietnam, some "upper class

enemies" were executed outright, but many more were sent off to "reeducation camps." After being allowed to see one of these camps because of his own anti-war credentials, a *Le Monde* correspondent termed it, *"Le Goulag Vietnamien."* Hundreds of thousands of former South Vietnamese government and military personnel died in these camps and tens of thousands perished in the "New Economic Zones."

The UN High Commissioner for Refugees had estimated that several hundred thousand South Vietnamese who fled their country in overcrowded and unseaworthy boats in search of freedom drowned or died of thirst or starvation, and one can only estimate how many men were forced to watch as their wives and young daughters were gang-raped by pirates (and then often killed or carried off never to be seen again). The total deaths directly attributable to "liberation" in South Vietnam and Cambodia certainly exceeded two million.

The "peace movement" so-called quest for "human rights" in Vietnam based on the belief that the Vietnamese people would settle their own affairs and human rights would flourish, was a fantasy. The protesters were not heroes; they caused much death and destruction by their selfish, irrational antics.

The human rights group, Freedom House, ranks every country in the world annually on the basis of its political and civil liberties. For decades after "liberation" the Socialist Republic of Vietnam was at the bottom of the "Dirty Dozen" or "Worst of the Worst" lists. At one point it was described as "less free than China, about as free as North Korea." This was the legacy of the American "peace movement."

Vietnam Was A Just War

Some writers, media members, and so-called historians still present distorted history and lies about the Vietnam War calling it "orthodox history" claiming with glee that "America lost the Vietnam War," that the war was illegal and emphasize the 58,000 dead, or they disregard the fact that Vietnam veterans saved the rest of South-East Asia from Communist domination. The Vietnam War was truly a fight for the freedom of the South Vietnamese. The slogan, "Support our troops," should have applied to Vietnam veterans.

Approximately 3.4 million Americans served "in theater" (off the coastal waters or flying from Thailand) during the Vietnam War; however, research (based on Veterans Administration claims and other documentation) indicates that approximately 13 million Americans claim to have served "in theater" during the war. A Vietnam era veteran's service in Germany, Korea, or CONUS should be acknowledged and appreciated, but it is NOT service in Vietnam or its theater of operations. Dysfunctional Vietnam veterans, those who did not serve honorably, veterans ignorant about the reasons for the war, or those who are not proud of their service often perpetuate the negatives of Vietnam veterans' service.

All veterans want to have their service recognized and appreciated, but Vietnam veterans were denied this. The very best way to honor Vietnam veterans is to tell the truth about their service in war. The truth about Vietnam veterans service in the Vietnam War is—that the war was legal—that most Vietnam veterans volunteered and are proud of their service—that Vietnam veterans actually fought for freedom and their service was extraordinary—that U.S. forces won the 1968 Tet Offensive—that My Lai and other acts of misconduct were exceptions and not the rule—that the U.S. won the Vietnam War in 1973—that Congress broke its promise to continue logistical support to South Vietnam and allowed the North to renew attacks and prevail—and that Vietnam veterans are true heroes.

It is appropriate to honor the dead, but the best way to Honor living Vietnam veterans is to tell about the misrepresentations of the media and anti-war movement, their fighting for freedom, and their extraordinary service defending the people of South Vietnam. Honor the living Vietnam veterans. They'll appreciate it.

Colonel Joseph E. Abodeely, USA (Ret)

Appendix 2

LTC Robinson (later General Robinson), my battalion commander, had written complimentary words in my Officer Evaluation Report (OER) for 9 JAN to 10 MAR 68:

"As a rifle platoon leader, Lieutenant Abodeely has conducted many platoon size operations which include night ambushes, search and clear, search and destroy and every other basic tactical technique used by a platoon. In addition to these platoon-sized operations, he has also participated in innumerable company operations. Some of these operations include cross attachment with the ARVN troops.

Lieutenant Abodeely has unerring knowledge of basic infantry tactics. In addition to his exceptional basic knowledge, Lieutenant Abodeely has illustrated uncanny ability in land navigation and map orientation. This unique bit of perception appeared to give him an unusual ability at times to diagnose the enemy's intentions before they fully materialized...

I have observed, on numerous occasions, Lieutenant Abodeely's exceptional ability to react with equanimity and force under conditions of duress. He is a fearless leader and an inspiration to those who follow him. His primary concern, secondary to the mission, is the welfare and protection of those who follow him. Case in point, I watched him move into an open area, under heavy enemy fire, to pull two wounded men to safety..."

I came home from Vietnam in January 1969 to a hostile, ungrateful country; and in February, I entered law school for my last two years, while antiwar protests were going on all over the country. The antiwar protests really infuriated me. ***I never had as much responsibility for life and property as I did in Vietnam***, and, if there is a God, He saw to it that I survived and never lost a man.

During the 1969 October Moratorium at the law school, I spoke up and was mercilessly shouted down by the draft dodgers. I was mortified almost to tears as

I risked my life for my country, was almost killed several times, lead my troops to Khe Sanh, and kept all of my men alive in the bloodiest year of the war—all this to return to insults, jeering, and humiliation by draft-dodging law students.

I am proud to have served my country in the Vietnam War.

About the Author

Joe Abodeely was born in Tucson, Arizona in 1943. His education from grade school to Law School was in Tucson. A war was brewing, and he went to Vietnam in January 1968 as an Infantry Lieutenant. Assigned to the 1st Cavalry Division (Airmobile) AKA "the 1st Air Cavalry" (think *Apocalypse Now* or *We Were Soldiers*), he saw action during the bloodiest year of the war in the unit that saw the most combat. Upon returning home after his one-year tour, he was astonished and chagrined to see firsthand the public's disrespect for those risking their lives for their country.

Joe has practiced law for over 50 years, founded the Arizona Military Museum serving as its chief executive officer for over 40 years, presented annual dinners commemorating Vietnam veterans' service, and has been an outspoken advocate for those who honorably served in the Vietnam War. He is author of *Dear Mom and Dad, Love From Vietnam* (recipient of three Global E-book Awards), and *Vietnam Anti-War Movement: The*

Joe Abodeely

Great American Con Job, (recipient of 4 gold Global E-Book Awards and the Dan Poynter Legacy Award.) This is his third book.

Recommended Reading

Abodeely, Joe. *Dear Mom and Dad, Love from Vietnam*, Desert Bugle Press (2014).

Abodeely, Joe. *Vietnam Anti-War movement: The Great American Con Job*, Desert Bugle Press (2020).

Austin, Gloria. "Shaping Civilizations: The Role of the Horse in Human Societies," Equine Heritage Institute (2013). https://tinyurl.com/zjhbbbo

Banks, Herbert C. *1st Cavalry Division*, Turner Publishing Company (2002).

Beynon, Steve. "Army Mulls Returning to Gendered Fitness Standards over Complaints of 'Lopsided' ACFT" (2021) https://www.military.com/daily-news/2021/05/25/army-mulls-returning-gendered-fitness-standards-over-complaints-of-lopsided-acft.html

Bolger, Lt. General Daniel, USA (Ret). "1st Cav Rushed in During Operation Masher," *ARMY Magazine* (2021).

Boudreau, William H. "1st Cavalry Division Association, Division's history." www.first-team.us.

Brown, William F. *Our Vietnam Wars*, Volume 3. (2019).

Cox, Matthew. "Army Leaders Say ACFT 3.0 Remains Gender-Neutral, Despite Gender-Specific Evaluation Categories," (2021). https://www.military.com/daily-news/2021/03/22/army-leaders-say-acft-30-remains-gender-neutral-despite-gender-specific-evaluation-categories.html

Glen, John Mason. "Was America Duped at Khe Sanh?" (2018). https://

www.nytimes.com/2018/01/01/opinion/was-america-duped-at-khe-sanh.html

Hammel, Eric. *The Siege of Khe Sanh: An Oral History*, Warner Books (1989).

Huff, Ethan. "US Army ends gender neutral fitness test because female soldiers keep failing…Men and women are different after all," Freedom First Network. (2021). https://freedomfirstnetwork.com/2021/04/us-army-ends-gender-neutral-fitness-test-because-female-soldiers-keep-failing-men-and-women-are-different-after-all

Hunt, Luke. "The Vietnam War's Great Lie," The Diplomat (2018). https://thediplomat.com/2018/02/the-vietnam-wars-great-lie/

Ketcham, Sally Johnson, "Historic Furnishing Plan for the Dragoon Stable," U.S. Army Heritage and Education Center. (2017).

Lewis, John E. *The Mammoth Book of War Diaries and Letters*, editor, Carroll and Graf (1999).

Edited by Morgan, Speer and Michalson, Greg. *For Our Beloved Country*, Atlantic Monthly Press (1994).

Moyar, Mark. *Historians at War*, U.S. Marine Corps University, Quantico (Spring 2008).

Meyers, Major Quinn and Schneider, CWO4 Tom. "Special Ops Aviation Unit Hones Tactics in Desert," Association of the United States Army (2021). https://www.ausa.org/articles/special-ops-aviation-unit-hones-tactics-desert

Prados, John and Stubbe, Ray. *Valley of Decision: The Siege of Khe Sanh*, Dell Publishing (1991).

Shaw, Geoffrey. *The Lost Mandate of Heaven, The American Betrayal of Ngo Dinh Diem, President of Vietnam*, Ignatius Press (2015).

Vietnam Was A Just War

Stanton, Shelby L. *The 1st Cav in Vietnam, Anatomy of a Division*, Ballantine Books (1987).

Tolson, Lieutenant General John J. *Vietnam Studies—Airmobility 1961-1971*, Department of the Army, Washington (1973).

Credits

Front cover: ©Deposit Photos/Marzolino. Used with permission. ©iStockPhoto/razihusin. Used with permission.

Back cover: ©Deposit Photos/HorenkO. Used with permission.

p. viii. __. **"6 Presidents Who Served During the Vietnam War."** Adapted from https://www.thevietnamwar.info.

p. 33. __. **"Just War Theory."** Adapted from Wikipedia. Wikipedia contributors, Wikipedia.com. Accessed on 5/17/22. https://en.wikipedia.org/w/index.php?title=Just_war_theory&oldid=1087326070

p. 44. __. **"Mass dead at Hue after occupation."** 1968. In the aftermath of the recapture of Hue in 1968, the discovery of several mass graves of South Vietnamese citizens of Hue sparked a controversy that has not diminished with time. The official allied explanation was that during occupation of the city hostiles to the communists were executed. Later the press revealed 'revenge squads" against those who had assisted the communists. The truth may never be known. Pictures from History / CPA Media Pte Ltd. Alamy.com Image ID: 2B01FJ5. Used with permission.

p. 48. __. **"Army Airborne In Vietnam."** Ben Hoa, Vietnam: 1967. U.S. Army Airborne soldiers move through Viet Cong sniper fire toward the jungle after being dropped by Hueys in a rice field. Underwood Archives/UIG/Everett Collection. (4-War-VN-US-A-HA_4HR) UIGA010 XU933. Used with permission.

p. 54. __. **"Brigadier General Lê Minh Đảo."** Marked as "Courtesy of KBC-Hain Goai." Accessed on Wikipedia on 9/14/20 at https://en.wikipedia.org/wiki/L%C3%AA_Minh_%C4%90%E1%BA%A3o#/media/File:Xuanloc_18th.jpg. Public domain.

p. 124. __. **"Hue Citadel."** Vietnam tourist photo accessed 9/5/20 at http://hanoisplendidhotel.com/DAILY-TRIPS/Hue-City-1-Day-Top-choice.

p. 136 & 273. Cronkite, Walter. **"We are Mired in Stalemate,"** February 27, 1968. Excerpted from https://www.digitalhistory.uh.edu/active_learning/explorations/vietnam/cronkite.cfm.

p. 140. __. **"LZ Cà Lu (Stud)."** 1st Cav forces at Landing Zone Cà Lu (Stud), the staging area for Operation Pegasus. April 4, 1968. manhhai. Accessed on Creative Commons 9/14/20 at https://search.creativecommons.org/photos/ae6f9941-7589-4d14-9bb2-4165a1b22570. CC BY 2.0.

P. 140 USMC. **"B-52 strike near the U.S. Marine Corps base Khe Sanh."** 1968. USMC. Official U.S. Marine Corps photograph. Accessed on Creative Commons 5/17/22 at https://commons.wikimedia.org/wiki/File:B-52_strike_near_Khe_Sanh_1968.JPG. Public Domain.

p. 154. Dang, Phuoc Van. **"Operation Pegasus."** 1968. Associated Press photo. ID: 6804050711. Used with permission.

p. 156. Lutz, Robert. **"NVA mortar rounds and arms."** (2 photos.) Lutz personal collection. Used with permission.

p. 158. Author Photo. **"NVA Bugle captured near Khe Sanh."**

p,158. Alinamd. **"King Cobra."** ©Deposit Photos. Used with Permission.

Vietnam Was A Just War

p. 162. __. **"1st Air Cavalry Enters Khe Sanh."** 1968. Movie clip from U.S. Army combat camera. Public Domain.

p. 162. Nalty, Bernard C. **"The fight for Khe Sanh,"** Special Studies, Washington, DC: Office of Air Force History, United States Air Force, p. 100. Soldiers of the 1st Cavalry Division moving towards Khe Sanh Combat Base during Operation Pegasus. Accessed on Creative Commons on 9/5/20 at https://commons.wikimedia.org/wiki/File:Khe_Sanh_Operation_Pegasus_First_Cavalry.jpg. Public domain.

p. 167-169. Abodeely, Joseph. **Vietnam Diary Pages**. Author's collection.

p. 169-172. __. Author's collection of U.S. newspaper clippings.

p. 166. Author Photo. "**2nd Platoon D/2/7, 1st Cavalry Division (Airmobile)**."

p. 173. __. "1st Cavalry Bugles Way to Khe Sanh Marines." UPI, Wichta *Eagle*, Wichita, Kansas, April 8, 1968. Public domain.

p. 175. Tolson, Lieutenant General John J. *Vietnam Studies—Airmobility 1961-1971*, Department of the Army, Washington (1973).

p. 193. __. "The Battle of Khe Sanh," Wikipedia, the free encyclopedia (2021). Accessed June 7, 2022 at https://en.wikipedia.org/w/index.php?title=Battle_of_Khe_Sanh&oldid=1089410605

p. 214. __. **"Women Power."** Accessed on DameMagazine.com on June 5, 2014. 8/31/20 at: https://www.damemagazine.com/wp-content/uploads/2017/09/NY-MARCH-08-26-1971.jpg.

p. 214. Allen, Elmer, *People's World*. **"Seattle Chicanos lead Peace March,"** October 31, 1970. Part of the Harry Bridges Center for Labor Studies collection. Accessed on 9/20/20 at https://depts.washington.edu/civilr/mecha_photos.htm.

p. 214. St. John, Marmaduke. **"Viet Cong flags frame anti-Vietnam War protesters in Boston."** April, 1970. Note Black Panthers flag at upper right. Alamy.com. ID: B8XJ99. Used with permission.

p. 215. __. **"Zelfverbrandingen in Vietnam."** October 5, 1963. Spectators watch as flames engulf young Buddhist monk as he commits ritual suicide on Saigon's Market St. in this 10/5/1963 photo, protesting the government's religious policies. Self-immolation became a tactic of some demonstrators during the Vietnam War. Foter.com/manhhai. Accessed on Foter.com on 9/10/20 at https://foter.com/ffff/photo/25713334236/fd9865e401/. CC BY 2.0.

p. 216. __ . **"Black Panthers on steps of legislative building, Olympia, WA."** 1969. Washington State Archives, State Governors' Negative Collection, 1949-1975. (#4076.) On February 28, 1969, a group of Seattle Panthers led by Lt. Elmer Dixon gathered on the steps of the Capitol in Olympia to protest a bill that would make it a crime to exhibit firearms "in a manner manifesting an intent to intimidate others." In contrast to a California demonstration, they did not enter the building and they were not arrested. https://www.digitalarchives.wa.gov/Record/View/F4335BFEDE59686C55B7D39E38C1E07D. Public domain.

p. 216. Leffler, Warren K. **"Martin Luther King, Jr.,** head-and-shoulders portrait, facing right, at microphones, after? meeting with President Johnson to discuss civil rights, at the White House, 1963 / WKL." December 3, 1963. Library of Congress. RN: LC-DIG-ds-00836. CN: LC-U9- 10978-A-3. Accessed on 9/10/20 at https://www.loc.gov/pictures/item/2011648312/. No known restrictions on publication.

p. 217. __. **"Vietnam Veterans Against the War."** Chicago, October 25, 1971. Vietnam Veterans Against the War (VVAW), *The Veteran*, Fall, 2014. Photo titled "halgash_nixon_chi_3-15-74." Accessed on 9/20/20 at http://www.vvaw.org/veteran/article/?id=2867.

p. 217. Leffler, Warren K. **"Civil rights march on Washington, D.C.** / [WKL]." Washington D.C, August 28, 1963. A crowd of Blacks and Whites surround-

Vietnam Was A Just War

ing the Reflecting Pool and continuing to the Washington Monument. Library of Congress. RN: LC-DIG-ppmsca-03130. Call Number. LC-U9-10363-5. Accessed on 9/22/20 at https://www.loc.gov/pictures/resource/ppmsca.03130/. No known restrictions on publication.

p. 218. Kent State University News Service. **"National Guard personnel walking toward crowd near Taylor Hall, tear gas has been fired,"** Kent State University Libraries. Special Collections and Archives, accessed August 29, 2020, https://omeka.library.kent.edu/special-collections/items/show/1427. ID: 705/4-1-35. Used with permission

p. 218. Kent State University News Service. **"National Guard personnel wearing gas masks, holding rifles,"** Kent State University Libraries. Special Collections and Archives, accessed September 2, 2020, https://omeka.library.kent.edu/special-collections/items/show/1427. ID: 705/4-1-22. Used with permission.

p. 219. __. **"List of Protests" from Wikipedia.** Wikipedia contributors, Wikipedia.com. Accessed on 8/25/20. https://en.wikipedia.org/w/index.php?title=List_of_protests_against_the_VietnamWar&oldid=973365665.

p. 266. __. **Arizona Capital Veteran's Memorial.** Author's collection.

www.ingramcontent.com/pod-product-compliance
Lightning Source LLC
Chambersburg PA
CBHW070532010526
44118CB00012B/1113